The China Hands' Legacy

Ethics and Diplomacy

About the Book and Editor

A group of American Foreign Service officers and journalists in China during and after World War II—collectively known as "the China Hands"—were accused of disloyalty, and in some cases treason, for reporting on events as they saw them. Faced with the ethical dilemma of what a public official's responsibility is when one believes one's government's policy is wrong, these men and women wrote what they considered to be the truth. Forty years later, their celebrated experiences provide a case study for the exploration of larger questions about U.S. foreign policy, relations between the United States and East and Southeast Asia, and ethics and diplomacy. This volume combines the perspectives of former China Hands themselves looking back upon their personal experiences with those of noted scholars; together the two groups explore the China Hands' legacy and its meaning for the future.

Paul Gordon Lauren is director and professor of ethics and public affairs at the Mansfield Center at the University of Montana.

The China Hands' Legacy

Ethics and Diplomacy

edited by
Paul Gordon Lauren

Westview Press / Boulder and London

Copyright © 1987 by Westview Press, Inc.

Published in 1987 in the United States of America by Westview Press, Inc.; Frederick A. Praeger, Publisher; 5500 Central Avenue, Boulder, Colorado 80301

Library of Congress Cataloging-in-Publication Data
The China Hands' legacy.
  Bibliography: p.
  Includes index.
  1. United States—Foreign relations—China.
2. China—Foreign relations—United States. 3. Dip-
lomacy—Moral and ethical aspects. I. Lauren, Paul
Gordon.
E183.8.C5C475 1986   327.51073   86-11193
ISBN 0-8133-0224-2 (alk. paper)

Printed and bound in the United States of America

The paper used in this publication meets the requirements of the American National Standard for Permanence of Paper for Printed Library Materials Z39.48-1984.

10   9   8   7   6   5   4   3   2   1

for Maureen and Mike Mansfield

CONTENTS

ACKNOWLEDGMENTS

It gives me great pleasure to acknowledge all those individuals who contributed in one way or another to this volume. In addition to the contributors themselves, I extend gratitude

- for enthusiasm and leadership in design and implementation to Charles Hood;

- for conceptual and organizational support to James Lopach, Jack Mudd, Tom Huff, Mark Clark, and Ruth Patrick;

- for financial assistance from the Maureen and Mike Mansfield Center at the University of Montana and the Montana Committee for the Humanities;

- for encouragement and advice to Barbara Ellington, Libby Barstow, and Lauri Fults of Westview Press;

- for various forms of assistance to Neil Bucklew, Donald Habbe, Dan Smith, Don Spencer, Greg MacDonald, Karen Kaley, Margaret Kingsland, Steve MacKinnon, Patty Reksten, Jyl Hoyt, Chen Jiang, Lu Yutai, Susan Matule, Neile Graham, Kate Saenger, and Leota Fred;

- and, for patience, to my wife, Susan, and our daughters, Sandy and Jeanne.

Paul Gordon Lauren

1

The China Hands:
An Introduction

As 1950 began, Alger Hiss, an important and well-placed career diplomat of the United States, found himself the principal target of the House Committee on Un-American Activities, embroiled in a sensational trial. On January 21 he was convicted of perjury. Within a few days a major espionage case exploded before the public eye. In the United States Senate, hitherto unknown and freeswinging Republican Senator Joseph McCarthy sensed that the time might be politically ripe to accelerate his accusations against those Americans whom he regarded as being "soft" on Communists, loyal to the ideals and designs of communism, and responsible for "losing" China to Mao Tse-tung's Communist forces. On February 9, at a colorful Lincoln's Day dinner in Wheeling, West Virginia, McCarthy launched his attack and fired his now famous salvo by unashamedly proclaiming in public:

> Ladies and gentlemen, while I cannot take the time to name all the men in the State Department who have been named as active members of the Communist Party and members of a spy ring, I have here in my hand a list of 205—a list of names that were made known to the Secretary of State as being members of the Communist Party and who nevertheless are still working and shaping policy in the State Department.[1]

In the upheaval that followed, much of the attention of McCarthy and his many supporters focused upon the "China Hands," those individuals in the Foreign Service who had served in China and become experts on Chinese affairs during the preceding years. In the anti-Communist purge that followed, these diplomats and a number of journalists also with experience in China found themselves accused of "losing" China to the Communists, of being "card-carrying" members or "fellow travelers" of the Communist Party, and of practicing disloyalty and even treason against the United States for the reports they wrote and the conclusions they reached from China. During World War II they had reported the truth as they saw it: that regardless of what their own government wanted to hear, America's ally, Chiang Kai-shek, headed a corrupt regime lacking support among the Chinese people and likely to collapse in the face of growing Communist strength. They argued that this was not necessarily desirable for the United States, but that it was going to happen. When they were proven right, they were accused of having willed the event and of having contributed to the outcome.[2] Their case raised—and their legacy continues to raise—critical questions about modern Chinese-American relations, memory and historical consciousness, shifting political realities in war and peace, utopianism and the modern state, intercultural communication and understanding, the function of the press in free societies, and the ethical problems that arise in the conduct of diplomacy.

China and America

China has always seemed to have a special allure and attraction for Americans. Its land, long history, and fascinating multitudes of people have aroused interest, curiosity, sympathy, and greed, among many other reactions. China's mysteries and philosophies attracted scholars thirsty for knowledge. Its markets, resources, and financial opportunities, as Raymond Wylie and Immanuel Hsu suggest in Chapter 3 attracted merchants and investors hungry for profits. China's people attracted missionaries ardent to help and to win souls. Its location attracted soldiers anxious for strategic footholds in Asia. And, after the successful revolution led by Sun Yat-sen against the old Ch'ing Dynasty and then the creation of the Republic of China in 1912, as Akira Iriye observes in Chapter 4, the country attracted the attention of political and social reformers eager to bring the benefits of democracy and modern technology to an ancient land.

This attraction certainly did not diminish with the subsequent rise of political parties in China. Indeed, the creation in 1912 of the Kuomintang, or Nationalist People's Party, and the formation in 1921 of the Kungch'antang, or Communist Party, attracted even greater attention. Both parties wanted to modernize China, to mobilize the Chinese people in political life, and to create new forms of government for the future; for a time, they actually worked with each other to achieve common objectives. This uneasy alliance was broken in 1927 when the leader of the Kuomintang, Chiang Kai-shek, bolted and established the Nationalist government of China. Although initially deeply committed to the principles of democracy and the people's livelihood, like many other revolutionaries in history the Nationalists and Chiang increasingly became concerned with preservation of their own wealth and power. With the growth of secret police surveillance, censorship, the suppression of opposition, starvation in the countryside, and corruption, Chiang's government found itself steadily abandoned by the intellectuals, losing the support of the peasants and their perception of his "Mandate from Heaven" to govern, and seriously challenged by the Chinese Communists under the leadership of Mao Tse-tung. In response to Mao's challenge, Chiang launched a series of extermination campaigns against the Communists, forcing them by 1934 to undertake the now legendary Long March of more than 6,000 miles through numerous perils and to transfer their headquarters far away to the arid, sunbaked hills of Yenan in North China.

In the midst of this dramatic contest for the control of China's destiny, the Japanese decided to take advantage of the internal disunity and expand their control over Chinese territory. The expansion started during 1931 when military forces from Japan overran most of the key Chinese positions in South Manchuria. Shortly thereafter, the Japanese staged an assault upon Shanghai. Incidents continued during the following years, then exploded in 1937 when serious fighting broke out between Chinese and Japanese troops at the Marco Polo Bridge near Peking. The resulting Sino-Japanese War struck at the very foundations of the Nationalist regime, significantly draining away resources and energies. At the same time, it also provided unprecedented opportunities for the Chinese Communists to increase their revolutionary strength and influence in the countryside. Both the Nationalists and the Communists, however, understood that this external threat to China endangered them more than their internal struggle for power and hence agreed to a program of National Unity whereby the Communists would place their troops under Nationalist command to fight the common enemy. As a result of this agreement the supreme commander, Generalissimo Chiang Kai-shek, possessed at least nominal control over all Chinese forces, but he knew that in order to survive he needed vast amounts of American assistance.

In the past, Americans always had given considerable aid to the Chinese, but this had appeared largely in the form of missionary assistance, private philanthropy, and person-to-person or group-to-group contributions. With the attacks upon China by the Japanese, however, assistance quickly came to be official as the U.S. government sought to support the government of China in order to provide a check upon Japan in Asia. Chiang made it clear that his was the only officially recognized government of China and that he thus intended to remain the sole channel through which American support would go to the Chinese. The United States complied and began providing funds, making loans, and even clandestinely establishing an air force known as the Flying Tigers in Burma and Yunnan under Claire Chennault to bring military supplies to China. When the Japanese launched their surprise attack upon Pearl Harbor, and the United States entered World War II, what had been a trickle of assistance became a veritable flood of financial, material, and technical aid. With this, the two countries joined as allies, and their futures became very closely intertwined. But as scholar John King Fairbank writes of this development: "Unfortunately our ally the Nationalist Government was by 1942 already well advanced in that process of decline. . . . From the very beginning of our wartime alliance, American officials found themselves dealing with an ineffective administration, too debilitated by its domestic problems to respond to foreign stimuli. Trying to aid it, we became entangled in its decline and fall."[3]

This entanglement began almost immediately. In order to coordinate the use of such aid and military policy, President Franklin Roosevelt sent General Joseph ("Vinegar Joe") Stilwell to China as the commanding general of U.S. Forces in the China-Burma-India Theater and as Chiang's chief of staff. Stilwell was the army's China specialist. He could both read and speak Chinese, had traveled widely throughout the country, and had been the American military attaché in Peking during the first years of China's war with Japan. Stilwell's assignment was to coordinate the distribution of military aid, to break the blockade of China by cutting his way through the Japanese occupying army in Burma, to modernize and retrain China's armies to become a genuine fighting force, and, in the process, to defend Chiang and his government. All of this made Stilwell, in the words of one contemporary observer on the scene in China, a "jockey to a dying horse."[4]

It did not take Stilwell long to understand the impossible nature of his mission. When the war came, Roosevelt and the American people viewed Chiang as a precious ally, the master of a great Asian reservoir of manpower, the owner of a vast landmass from which a counterattack could be launched against Japan, and a democratic leader beloved by his countrymen. Yet, once in China again, it quickly became apparent to Stilwell that China had a government racked with corruption and incompetence and a dictatorial political leader despised by many of his own people. Stilwell watched Chiang deploy 200,000 of his best fighting troops, not against the Japanese as he had promised, but in a blockade against the Chinese Communists. He saw Chiang beg Americans for more and more aid and then hoard what was forthcoming for his own purposes rather than use it in war. He listened to Chiang make promises about victories when he knew perfectly well that Nationalist forces suffered defeats. Declared Stilwell in extreme frustration and bluntness, "The trouble in China is simple: We are allied to an ignorant, illiterate, superstitious peasant son of a bitch."[5]

For Stilwell, this terrible situation became even worse. Chiang insisted upon issuing his military orders without any effort at consultation. At times he simply refused to talk with Stilwell. On other occasions he deliberately tried to obstruct cooperation. Chiang strongly opposed any suggestion, for example, that Stilwell be allowed to at least establish some contact with the Chinese Communist armies in order to utilize their troops in the fight against Japan. Chiang also began to suggest to the United States that Stilwell should be recalled. "What Stilwell was beginning to learn," writes Theodore White, who personally witnessed these events, ". . . was

that all war at its supreme level is dominated by politics and that
no fighting army could be created in China without changing the
politics of China."[6]

The political dimensions of the war were evident in other ways
as well. Chiang and his government, for example, knew that massive
American aid was essential for their survival and thus exerted great
effort and expended enormous funds to influence the American
political process. They used paid lobbyists, their own officials, and
a variety of other allies who had the leverage of wealth and influence
to recruit friends, engender sympathy, and encourage the United
States to increase its assistance to the Nationalists. Many of these
supporters worked together in a loosely organized confederation
known as the China Lobby. The power of this group probably never
was as great as either its defenders or opponents claimed, but its
members included several extremely wealthy and influential Americans ranging from textile importer Alfred Kohlberg to Henry Luce,
the publisher of *Time-Life*, to Pittsburgh industrialist Frederick McKee.
The lobby took particular pride in the access it possessed to
Republican senators and congressmen like Joseph McCarthy, Patrick
McCarran, and Walter Judd. These men, in turn, were strategically
placed to provide assistance for Chiang—and to provide formidable
opposition to those who might not agree that the Nationalists deserved
full American support.[7]

In order to maintain this political support within the United States,
Chiang also tried to control American journalists in China by means
of travel restrictions and censorship. As Charles Hood observes in
Chapter 8, Chiang's officials carefully attempted to watch where
members of the press went, what they heard, and what they reported.
Theodore White, interestingly enough, found himself a part of this
process while he temporarily served as an adviser to the Chinese
Ministry of Information. In a revealing passage in his own colorful
autobiography, he writes:

> I was employed . . . to manipulate American public opinion. The
> support of America against the Japanese was the government's
> one hope for survival; to sway the American press was critical. It
> was considered necessary to lie to it, to deceive it, to do anything
> to persuade America that the future of China and the United States
> ran together against Japan. That was the only war strategy of the

Chinese government . . . and my job was to practice whatever deception was needed to implement the strategy.[8]

This propaganda effort may have worked within the United States among those removed from Chinese affairs, but it proved to be singularly ineffective among many of those Americans who in their official or professional capacity resided in China and saw Chiang and the Nationalists for themselves. These included military commanders like General Stilwell, the American ambassador Clarence Gauss and his China Hand political advisers from the Foreign Service, and a large number of journalists, among others. As one newspaperman on the scene rather imaginatively described it, Chiang and his government were like the panel of a modern switchboard. When one pushed the buttons, the lights winked, but the wires in the back led nowhere and the panel "did not connect to the operations system. And the parade of American advisers, aid masters, and generals who . . . [came] to help all exploded in impotent fury when they finally realized the switchboard did not work."[9]

In the midst of this fury and confusion, the China Hands faced a number of serious ethical dilemmas. Individually and collectively they had to deal with the difficult problem of what public officials should do when they believe their government is wrong. On the one hand, they had a clear responsibility to tell the truth the way they saw it. Regardless of how unpleasant the facts might be, their government needed accurate information and assessments. As Melby describes it in his chapter, ideally any Foreign Service officer "should always report what he sees, hears, smells, and feels, preferably rounded off with his interpretations and recommendations." To do so, however, runs serious risks of contradicting official policy and thus appearing disloyal, of harming relations with an ally during time of war and thus seeming treasonous, or of placing one's own career in serious jeopardy. As Davies observes in his chapter, a Foreign Service officer in this situation faces a choice either to "remain silent" or to "speak out about his misgivings and suggest alternative policies, knowing that he runs serious personal risks in so doing." Davies, Melby, and the other China Hands chose to speak out and to tell the truth the way they saw it.

"Truth," however, is not always as easy to determine as one might want to believe. As all of the following chapters indicate, what active participants in the world of diplomacy determine to be the empirical truth is frequently conditioned by a number of factors. Wylie and Hsu, for example, stress the importance of geographical perspective and the limitations of vision imposed by local conditions. Melby emphasizes the role played by ideology and subjective judgments. May discusses the importance of domestic factors and ethical notions of political loyalty. And Davies is quick to remind us that diplomats must always face the difficulty of making reports and hazarding estimates based upon insufficient evidence, because the facts are never all available at the time of need.

Yet another ethical problem for diplomats arises over the question of establishing contacts. The fulfillment of their classical responsibility to gather accurate information and report it to their home government requires that they gather intelligence from foreign sources. But are some sources clearly acceptable while others are not? In times of war, for example, is it ethically better to maintain contact only with allies, even if it is known that they are corrupt and engage in censorship, or is it more ethically sound to seek accurate information wherever it can be found, regardless of the source? Again, as Davies suggests in Chapter 2, "if a Foreign Service officer must sever connections with everyone, American and foreign, about whom there has been or may be a derogatory report, then he will, of necessity, live in a useless vacuum." Consequently, the China Hands established whatever contacts they could with the Chinese Communists.

These two problems of reporting accurate information and gathering it where they could placed the American China Hands at serious odds with their Chinese Nationalist allies and Chiang's supporters (including those in the China Lobby within the United States). Indeed, after two years, Stilwell found himself spending seemingly more time in political battles with the Nationalists than in military combat against the Japanese. Time and time again he had been checked by Chiang in his efforts to establish contacts with the Communists and to assist them in fighting Japan. Stilwell's efforts remained unsuccessful until the summer of 1944 when Vice President Henry Wallace placed enough political pressure on Chiang for authority to establish the so-called Dixie Mission of American observers to Mao's headquarters in Yenan.[10] The price that Stilwell paid for this victory, however, was his job. After this, Chiang announced that he could no longer work with the man, claimed that he "was in conspiracy with the Communists" to overthrow the Nationalist government, and insisted that Stilwell be relieved of his command in China.[11] Roosevelt, reluctant to push Chiang too far, complied and recalled Stilwell. Shortly thereafter, Ambassador Gauss resigned. To replace Stilwell, Washington sent General Albert Wedemeyer; and to replace Gauss, the president sent General Patrick J. Hurley.

To his defenders, Hurley appeared the embodiment of American patriotism, a man who belonged in the same league as George Washington and Robert E. Lee.[12] To his many detractors, Hurley seemed instead a "hustler," an "ignoramus," a "liar," and a man who possessed some of the characteristics of a "snake-oil salesman."[13] Although a former corporate lawyer in Oklahoma and secretary of war under President Herbert Hoover, he nevertheless retained a number of colorful eccentricities such as his disconcerting habit, when the mood struck him, of emitting bloodcurdling Choctaw war whoops. Hurley knew little about Chinese affairs and largely distrusted those who did. But none of this seemed to bother Roosevelt who wanted to secure bipartisanship for the war effort and thus rather incredibly named the Republican Hurley as the American ambassador to China.

At this same time, Roosevelt asked Mike Mansfield to undertake a special mission to China. Although only a freshman congressman, Mansfield had taught Far Eastern history at the University of Montana, spoken frequently for the Asian and Pacific theaters of the war for the Foreign Affairs Committee, and possessed some personal experience in Asia. Roosevelt apparently wanted an independent assessment of the Chinese situation in the midst of all the turmoil and believed that Mansfield could provide it. After briefings from John Carter Vincent from the Department of State, interviews with Frank McNaughton of *Time,* and luncheons with Dr. H. H. Kung, Chiang Kai-shek's brother-in-law, Mansfield left for China in November 1944.

Upon arrival, he set about to visit with as many individuals as he could. He talked with officers such as U.S. Generals Claire Chennault and Albert Wedemeyer to hear about military needs for the prosecution of the war. He met with Chinese businessmen in Chungking to learn their assessments of economic conditions. He visited with Chiang Kai-shek, his Foreign Minister T. V. Soong, his adviser Chiang Meng-lin, and his Minister of War Chen Cheng and was told that they needed more assistance and that they intended to institute reforms in China once the war ended. He spoke with China Hands John Paton Davies and Arthur Ringwalt about political conditions. He talked with journalists like Theodore White who told him about difficulties with Henry Luce distorting information about Chiang in order to fit editorial policy.[14] Mansfield also met with Hurley, summarizing his meeting with these words: "We had a very long talk. He talked for two hours and forty-seven minutes and I talked for thirteen minutes. . . ."[15]

When Mansfield returned to the United States he wrote a lengthy report to President Roosevelt discussing the details of his trip and providing a number of candid assessments about the Chinese situation. "It appears to me," he stated, "that as of this date, China's house has a leaky roof and a shaky foundation. Whether or not that house can be put in order is a question mark." He criticized the "spirit of sanctimoniousness" among the Communists, but believed that "they seem to have evolved a system of government which is quite democratic." Mansfield used his strongest words against the Nationalist government. It was, he said, "hated more every day. . . . It is corrupt. It speaks democratically but acts dictatorially. The worst censorship in the world is located in Chungking . . . [It] is afraid of the will of the people, has lost much of its popular support, and will not allow any of its power to be used in the way of agrarian reforms." He nevertheless believed that Chiang was probably the only man who could carry China through the war, even though he concluded that both the Nationalists and the Communists were "more interested in preserving their respective parties . . . than in carrying on the war in Japan."[16] After giving the report to Roosevelt, Mansfield sent a copy to Secretary of State Edward Stettinius, asking him to turn it over to John Carter Vincent, and complimenting China Hands like John Paton Davies as part of "a fine group of men representing our country in China."[17]

Mansfield's China Mission Report brought him widespread national attention (and later criticism from McCarthy), but it appears to have had little immediate effect upon Roosevelt during the last weeks of his life or upon Hurley who decided as early as November 1944 to take matters into his own hands. In order to obtain cooperation from both the Nationalists and the Communists, he flew unannounced into Yenan to negotiate some kind of an agreement. Here he presented a rather remarkable proposal that the Nationalists and the Communists work together for the unification of all military forces in China, that a coalition government be formed, that foreign aid be distributed equitably to all anti-Japanese forces, that all political parties be legally recognized, and that they create in China "a government of the people, for the people, and by the people," as Davies describes in Chapter 2. Mao Tse-tung and Chou En-lai signed the agreement for the Communists, but when Hurley took it to Chungking, Chiang refused. When the Nationalists then changed the conditions, Mao became furious and, at that, Hurley flew into a rage.[18] He then resolved that America should give all of its support to the anti-Communist Nationalists. As one reporter who watched all this wrote: "The back-slapping Patrick Hurley . . . tried to settle the deep-rooted Kuomintang-Communist troubles with a twist of his own hand. He failed, and then threw all support to Chiang with no questions asked. This support encouraged Chiang to resort to outright warfare. . . ."[19]

Hurley, of course, cannot be blamed for Chiang's behavior. More-over, he certainly may have meant well in his attempt to find reconciliation. But single-handedly, and without any guidance, he certainly could not have unraveled the complex political, ideological, economic, and military knots that entangled wartime China. When he failed, Hurley blamed others. He had the professional China Hands who still remained near him removed from China, muzzled his staff, ordered that nothing be forwarded to Washington unless he himself initialed it, and declared that no unfavorable reports about Chiang Kai-shek would be sent at all. Henceforth, he announced, American policy would be one of unqualified support of the Nationalists and of Chiang.[20]

Hurley staunchly enforced this position as long as he remained in a position of authority. When the war ended, however, he decided to take a leave in the United States and immediately began accusing others for his mistakes. In particular, he singled out the China Hands. "The professional Foreign Service men," he charged, "sided with the Chinese Communist armed party. . . . [and] continuously advised the Communists that my efforts in preventing the collapse of the National Government did not represent the policy of the United States."[21] President Harry Truman accepted his letter of resignation the day after it was offered and then appointed General George C. Marshall as his special envoy to China.

But, at the end of the war, what was occurring in China was well beyond Marshall's or anyone else's control. Once the common threat of Japan disappeared in August of 1945, whatever tenuous forces of unity that had existed crumbled into dust. Despite Marshall's valiant attempts to find a lasting cease-fire, neither the Nationalists nor the Communists trusted each other or were prepared to give up their own hopes for eventual control of all of China. Mao and his Communists quickly strengthened themselves through the capture, with Soviet assistance, of surrendered Japanese arms and then rapidly secured positions in North China. Chiang and his Nationalists wanted to regain their power bases in the coastal centers, and the United States helped to transport more than one-half million of their troops to accomplish this objective. Yet, by this time, the Nationalists could not govern effectively. The disruption of China's economy, under way for a century, had suffered enormously from years of warfare, and the government faced financial difficulties, including spiraling inflation that it lacked the resources, methods, and will to overcome. Increased taxes, military conscription, graft, looting, and the subsequent loss of moral prestige simply compounded all these problems, and more and more people became prepared to turn against Chiang and his government.[22]

The Chinese Civil War raged from 1946 to 1949 and tore the country apart. During this time the United States openly poured in well over two billion dollars of financial assistance alone for the Nationalists, while the Soviets clandestinely helped the Chinese Communists. At the beginning, Chiang's armies numbered approximately three million men, while those of Mao approached one million. But poor leadership, jealousies, corruption, demoralization, and desertion steadily eroded the Nationalist armies. By contrast, the Communist forces appeared dynamic, cohesive, and disciplined, and by 1948 they overran Manchuria and then pushed southward into the heart of China. With these victories, there soon emerged a steady shift in the balance of power toward the Chinese Communists. In January 1949, Nanking, Tientsin, and Peking surrendered to Mao's forces. During April they crossed the Yangtze River and by May entered Shanghai. Other cities fell to the Communists as well, and by October 1949 they triumphantly could raise the Red flag over

Tien An Men Square in Peking and proclaim the creation of the Chinese People's Republic.

To have China fall into the hands of a Communist government seemed to many Americans to be a national disaster of the first magnitude. Their idealized ally, Chiang Kai-shek, had been humiliated and forced to flee to the island of Taiwan, while his long-standing opponent, Mao Tse-tung, emerged triumphant. By this time the Soviets had taken over Eastern Europe and now the Chinese Communists controlled the largest single national landmass in all Asia. How could the United States as the most powerful nation on earth, they asked, possibly have "lost" China? To them, the only answer that appeared to offer a satisfactory explanation was treachery and conspiracy: that important American policymakers had been anti-Chiang and therefore pro-Communist. For them, the guilty could be found in the Department of State and especially among that group already identified by Hurley as the professional Foreign Service officers known as the China Hands.

The China Hands

The bitter critics of American postwar foreign policy focused much of their deep resentment and anger upon the Department of State. Had this not been the organization, they asked, that allowed the "frittering away" of wartime victory, Soviet expansionism into Eastern Europe and the Soviet stranglehold on Berlin, the creation of the United Nations and its efforts to impose "world government," and the "loss" of China to Mao Tse-tung's Communist forces? Hence, they charged that the Department was a "veritable nest of Communists, fellow travelers, homosexuals, effete Ivy League intellectuals, and traitors."[23]

Stung by these charges, anxious to detect any genuine breaches of security, and under political pressure to take some form of action, the Truman administration initiated a series of loyalty investigations into various branches of the federal government, but especially into the Department of State. The process actually began under Secretary of State James Byrnes as early as 1945 and 1946 and resulted in the screening of 341 "disapprovals." Of these, 2 were discharged and 281 were, in the words of the department, "removed through various types of personnel action."[24] At the end of January 1947, the State Department disclosed that 40 employees had been dismissed for "close connections or involvement" with foreign powers, and by June, 10 more were dismissed as "potential security risks."[25]

These measures did little to quiet the critics, particularly as they simultaneously watched the continuing deterioration of the Nationalist regime and Chiang Kai-shek. Dean Acheson, who became secretary of state in 1949, sought to head off further criticism of the department. But his keen intellect and suave mannerisms often offended congressmen, as did his private description of them as "primitives," as May observes in Chapter 5. Anticipating that Chiang was now on the verge of collapse and defeat, the Department of State asked diplomat John Melby to produce a special collection of historical documents known as the China White Paper. In his introduction to the sensational volume, Acheson looked at the record and declared:

> The unfortunate but inescapable fact is that the ominous result of the civil war in China was beyond the control of the government of the United States. Nothing that this country did or could have done within the reasonable limits of its capabilities could have changed that result; nothing that was left undone by this country has contributed to it. It was the product of internal Chinese forces, forces which this country tried to influence but could not.[26]

This only seemed to antagonize the largely Republican critics more, for they argued that such statements were merely self-serving justifications of Democratic administrations guilty of treason themselves.

This series of attacks escalated into Armageddon for the Department of State when China finally "fell" and when McCarthy launched his purge against presumed traitors. Fearful and insecure as a result of the frightening gains of Communists in the Cold War (now especially in Asia), many Americans fell victim to a natural desire to find answers and scapegoats for the setbacks. Into this feverish setting stepped McCarthy with his January 1950 claim that he held in his hands the names of 205 "active members of the Communist Party and members of a spy ring," all of whom worked in the Department of State.[27] This charge set into motion the phenomenon John Melby discusses in his chapter, known as

"McCarthyism," as a result of which there began a full-scale assault against the China Hands.

After much political wrangling, Truman finally authorized the members of a special Senate Foreign Relations subcommittee chaired by Senator Millard Tydings to scrutinize the files of the Department of State. McCarthy responded by saying that this would prove absolutely nothing since the files would surely be "raped" before they ever reached the Senate. Both the attorney general and the Federal Bureau of Investigation (FBI), however, confirmed to the subcommittee that the files were complete and that a full investigation could begin. After more than thirty days of extensive hearings, the members of the subcommittee felt compelled to issue a public report and in July 1950, as Melby states, concluded that McCarthy's allegations represented an effort "to inflame the American people with a wave of hysteria and fear" and constituted "the most nefarious campaign of half-truths and untruths in the history of this republic." Yet, such judgments and subsequent public expressions of confidence in the Foreign Service seemed to have little effect upon McCarthy and his followers who dismissed them as self-serving statements from Democrats and thus refused to give up. The names of the employees from the Department of State, especially the China Hands, now had been publicized, and their future was to be dark.

The China Hands, as both Melby and Iriye observe in their chapters, found themselves caught in a maelstrom of shifting external and domestic political forces. Prior to 1949, Americans and Chinese had been accustomed to viewing their relationship as something special, a unique instance of friendship and interdependence. Almost overnight, however, with the victory of the Chinese Communists and the emerging Cold War, it was as if both countries wanted to eradicate all memories of the recent past. Thus, the advocacy by the China Hands of cooperation with Mao (in part to check the power of the Soviet Union in Asia) no longer fit into official policy. In addition, domestic political forces within the United States came to see those who had established ties with the Chinese Communists during World War II as somehow contaminated and disloyal. The results of these shifting forces can be seen in the fates of China Hands like John Service, John Carter Vincent, and John Paton Davies all accused of "losing" China to the Communists.

One of the most prominent among the China Hands was John Service. Born in 1901 of missionary parents serving the YMCA in Chengtu, China, he grew up knowing the country well. Service attended first grade in the United States while his mother and father were on home leave, but then returned to China the next year. The remaining years of his youth were spent in China where he became fluent in Chinese. Service traveled to the United States again to attend Oberlin College where he was captain of both the track and cross-country teams. After graduation he embarked upon a career in the Foreign Service. His first assignment was in the consulate at Shanghai where he worked for Clarence Gauss, a man who eventually would become the American ambassador to China and who later would say under oath: "I don't know of any officer in my whole thirty-nine years of service who impressed me more than Jack Service. . . ."[28] Throughout his career, he served in a number of other Chinese cities—including Kunming, Peking, Chungking, and Yenan. When the Japanese isolated Peking in 1937, Service volunteered to escort a party of Americans out of the city toward the relative safety of Tientsin. Later, as the Japanese moved farther and farther into the interior of China, he was sent to join the embassy staff in Chungking as a political adviser. Once the Americans entered World War II, his job, like all others in the office, was to help persuade all Chinese forces—Nationalists and Communists alike—to vigorously prosecute the war.

At that time the United States knew a great deal about Chiang Kai-shek and his Nationalists, for they had worked with them for several years, and the China Lobby at home was always quick to provide additional information if necessary. Yet, they hardly knew anything about Mao Tse-tung's Communists and had little idea about their numbers and strength, their long-range plans, or their degree of support in the countryside. To correct this problem, Service was assigned to find out all he could about the Communists and was posted as the first Foreign Service member of the Dixie Mission to the Communist "capital" of Yenan in 1944. From this remarkable vantage point, Service produced a series of historically significant political reports that no less an authority than George Kennan was later to describe as "an absolutely outstanding job of reporting."[29] Here, he reported events as he saw them: that Chiang was not the embodiment of China, that the Nationalist government was corrupt and in crisis, that the Communists had built up popular support of a magnitude and depth that made their elimination impossible, and that Mao's followers were likely to become the dominant force in China within a comparatively short time.[30] He certainly was not alone in these assessments, and when he and the several other diplomats sent to Yenan committed their thoughts to writing in an urgent message directly to the Department of State, Hurley exploded. "I know who drafted that telegram: Service," shouted Hurley. "I'll get that son of a bitch if it's the last thing I do."[31]

It took Hurley and his supporters several years to "get" Service, but they did. When he was replaced by General George C. Marshall, Hurley wasted no time in accusing Service of sabotage against the Nationalists, disloyalty to the United States, and treason for disclosing secret Allied plans to the Communists. In 1945 the Federal Bureau of Investigation arrested Service for allegedly violating the Espionage Act by giving classified information to the journal *Amerasia*. The Department of Justice submitted the case to a federal grand jury that, by a vote of 20 to 0, subsequently refused to indict Service, who acknowledged that he perhaps had been indiscreet with individuals who he believed were legitimate journalists but maintained that he was certainly not guilty of conspiracy or treason. Service then found himself subjected to four separate investigations by the Department of State between 1946 and 1948. Each time he was found innocent of any wrongdoing. But it did not stop there, for under pressure from McCarthy and his supporters, he received a summons in 1951 to appear before the Loyalty Review Board, a superagency for determining the fitness of government employees. The board determined that it need not confine itself to merely evaluating the findings of lower bodies like the Department of State's own Loyalty Security Board (the Supreme Court later would rule against this action) and could judge cases *de novo* by considering new evidence. With this they concluded that there was reasonable doubt as to the loyalty of John Service. Within hours of this decision, Dean Acheson fired him. Twenty years later it would bring tears to Service's eyes to recall how many people (including John Paton Davies and John Melby) turned up to comfort him. But he had been fired—banished from his profession, publicly humiliated, and terminated without pension.[32]

Referring to this action, however, Ernest May argues in his chapter that we need to be careful to recognize Acheson's ethical dilemmas as well as those of Service and of the other China Hands. Acheson certainly regarded himself as a man who acted on principle rather than mere political expediency and who surely would have answered that it was his duty to protect legitimate dissent within the Foreign Service. But he also faced the fact that some of the China Hands did not command solid confidence within the Foreign Service as a whole, and that the apparent majority of the elected representatives of the American people believed that the reporting of the China Hands encouraged erroneous policies. For these reasons, claims May, Acheson acted on what he believed were sound ethical principles, in the end firing Service and then turning to the other China Hands as well.

Another victim of the purge of the China Hands was John Carter Vincent. Born in 1900 in Kansas and then raised in Georgia, he entered the Foreign Service after college graduation. Vincent received his first position in Changsha, China, where he, too, distinguished himself in shepherding Americans in danger to safety. In due course he was sent to Peking for language training. Subsequent assignments sent him to Hankow, Swatow, Mukden, Nanking, and Dairen. During the war he found himself stationed in Chungking as the counselor of the American embassy, and thus working for Ambassador Gauss. In this capacity he, like many others, visited with the leaders of both the Nationalists and the Communists and formed a number of judgments about conditions in China. He accordingly advised Washington that the United States should not become overly concerned about Chiang's threats to pull out of the war if his continual demands for ever-more aid were not granted. This advice did not put him in the good graces of Hurley or of Alfred Kohlberg, one of the leaders of the China Lobby, who accused Vincent of being one of that group who "planned to slowly choke to death and destroy the government of the Republic of China and build up the Chinese Communists for postwar success."[33]

In 1944 Vincent returned to the Department of State where he was appointed chief of the Division of Chinese Affairs and then director of Far Eastern Affairs, but his presence in Washington did not diminish the debate about his role in China. Indeed, even though the war ended, arguments about Vincent and China only intensified.

Republican Senator Styles Bridges charged that Vincent's "actions, advice, and recommendations" had been "coordinated with the steps outlined" in the "Program of the Communist International" and that he had approved "of the Communist program in China, opposition to the support of the Nationalist government, and furtherance of extension of the influence of Russia in China."[34] In 1951 and 1952, McCarran's Senate Internal Security Subcommittee also turned on Vincent, and he heard himself accused of being a card-carrying member of the Communist Party. These charges prompted even more investigations, especially by the Loyalty Review Board. In 1952 by a 3-to-2 vote, this panel ruled against him by noting his "studied praise of Chinese Communists and equally studied criticism of the Chiang Kai-shek government throughout the period when it was the declared and established policy of the Government of the United States to support Chiang Kai-shek's government." Their recommendation: "that the services of Mr. John Carter Vincent be terminated."[35] Within days of assuming office, Secretary of State John Foster Dulles followed this advice and forced Vincent into retirement.

The Chinese mainland also served as the literal cradle and the political grave of another China Hand, John Paton Davies. The son of American missionary parents, he was born in Kiating in the far western province of Szechwan. He attended the University of Wisconsin for two years and then returned to China to enroll at Yenching University on the outskirts of Peking. John Leighton Stuart, who in later years would become the American ambassador to China, was president of the university. Here Davies met Edmund Clubb, who would become a China Hand himself and would also later be forced into retirement by Dulles. Davies returned to the United States to finish his degree at Columbia and take the Foreign Service examinations. Within a short time of passing his tests, he was off again to China for a post at the American consulate in Kunming. By 1933 Davies went to Peking for additional language training and within two years was assigned to Mukden to observe the Japanese at their principal rail and commercial center in Manchuria. After the Sino-Japanese War began, he was transferred to Hankow where Chiang Kai-shek had established a temporary seat of government.

A new assignment took Davies to Washington to serve in the Department of State's Division of Far Eastern Affairs. He was there when the Japanese launched their attack on Pearl Harbor in December

1941. This attack brought the United States into World War II and Davies back to China. The department designated him second secretary to the embassy at Chungking, but actually detailed him to General Stilwell as a political adviser. In this capacity, he spent considerable time in both China and India, the latter being particularly important as a base from which to send military supplies to the Chinese. Travel on this assignment often proved to be extremely hazardous, requiring dangerous flights in military transports across the Hump of the Himalayas. On one such journey in 1943, the airplane lost an engine and when lightening the load did not help in the emergency, the pilot abandoned the craft and ordered everyone to parachute out. The remaining survivors spent the next month trying to make their way through jungles and other dangers to safety. Eric Sevareid, who accompanied Davies in this unexpected ordeal, recalled how impressed he had been by Davies's natural leadership and his "great reserves of moral courage."[36] Eleven years later when Davies was under attack in Washington, Sevareid gave this remarkable public testimony in a radio broadcast:

> After we emerged into India and the military reports were in, there was a move in the Air Force to decorate our diplomat for his outstanding personal conduct. I do not know if he ever received the decoration. But none of us in the strange party, I think, would have disputed the choice. For I thought then, as I think now, that if ever again I were in deep trouble, the man I would want to be with would be this particular man. I have known a great number of men around the world, under all manner of circumstances. I have known none who seemed more the whole man; none more finished a civilized product, in all that a man should be—in modesty and thoughtfulness, in resourcefulness and steady strength of character.[37]

Stilwell's assignments brought Davies not only into contact with immediate physical danger but with what would later become smoldering political dangers as well. Some of these entailed journeys to Washington designed to convey assessments about conditions in China concerning Chiang's war efforts, the lack of military successes against the Japanese, and the support of the Communists in the Chinese countryside. His reports and news briefings thus invariably brought him into conflict with the efforts of Chiang and his wife and their friends in the China Lobby who wanted to convey the impression that the Nationalists alone represented China, that they were scoring military victories, that they needed more assistance, and that Stilwell himself ought to be removed. When the war was over, these supporters of Chiang would not forget Davies.

Perhaps his most sensitive assignment while in China was to be sent to Yenan to learn what he could about the Communists. Stilwell knew little about the Chinese Communists but did know that there were certain immediate advantages to be gained by striking up some acquaintance with them. They were in a position to provide important military intelligence, supply significant numbers of combat troops with high morale to fight against the common enemy of Japan, assist in weather reporting, offer some perspective on the accuracy of Chiang's wartime reports, and help rescue American bomber crews who might have to bail out in areas under their control. For all these reasons, Davies was assigned to the Dixie Mission and told to go to Yenan and meet with the Chinese Communists. Accompanying him in October 1944 were John Emmerson, another China Hand, and Theodore White, a young journalist from *Time*.

This setting, as Davies writes in Chapter 2, "was extraordinary—assorted military and diplomatic officers housed, fed, and entertained by a revolutionary hierarchy which was readily accessible for discussion on almost any topic. We were thus able to view the future rulers of China closeup." Indeed, here he had the unique opportunity to learn the strengths and the weaknesses of the Chinese Communists, to discuss military strategy and capabilities, to consider postwar relationships between China and the United States, to talk about the intentions of the Soviet Union in Asia, and to personally assess the nature of the future Chinese leadership. One photograph, for example, shows Davies standing outside a simple dwelling typical of Yenan at the time, flanked on one side by Chou En-lai and Chu Teh and on the other by Yeh Chien-ying and Mao Tse-tung himself.[38]

At the end of his stay in Yenan, Davies wrote four major policy papers. One outlines the nature of Communists' military capabilities and the commitment of Chou En-lai and Chief of Staff Yeh Chien-ying to provide combat troops in the struggle against the Japanese. In another, entitled "How Red Are the Chinese Communists?" he reached the conclusion that politics rather than ideology would play the critical role in the future evolution of the party. In the memorandum, "The Chinese Communists and the Great Powers," Davies stated that the United States held the key to the future, arguing that more aid given exclusively to Chiang would increase the likelihood of a civil war and the probability of a protracted and costly Communist unification of China. He suggested that the United States consider ways to attract the Communists and to induce them away from any dependence upon the Soviet Union. Finally, in a paper entitled "Will the Communists Take Over China?" he offered the assessment that the Chinese Communists had done nothing but increase their popular support and the territory under their control during the several previous years while Chiang, in sharp contrast and despite all the American aid given to him, had only lost both popular backing and land. He therefore concluded that the future of China was likely to belong to Mao rather than Chiang.[39]

These observations did not sit well with Hurley who saw Davies, like the other China Hands of the Foreign Service, as an opponent of his plan to sustain the Nationalists and to arrange a unification of China under Chiang's supremacy in a coalition government. These thoughts were encouraged by T. V. Soong, Chiang's foreign minister, who wanted to replace Davies with someone less critical of the Nationalists and more sympathetic to increased aid for Chiang. Tensions increased to the point where little could be accomplished, and therefore, by mutual consent, a transfer out of China was arranged, and Davies received orders to work in the embassy in Moscow. When Davies went in to say goodbye to Hurley in January 1945, the ambassador turned on him and, according to eyewitness General Albert Wedemeyer, "accused Davies of being a Communist and of failing to support the directive of his country in support of the Chinese Nationalists. . . . Hurley said that he was going to have him kicked out of the State Department."[40]

Just when Davies thought he was safe from Hurley's personal attacks, the ambassador flew into Moscow on his way from Washington and London to Chungking. Hurley already had determined that Chiang should emerge supreme in any postwar Chinese government and that Joseph Stalin should support him, and he would not listen to those such as Davies who might contradict him. George Kennan, then deputy at the Moscow embassy, watched this whole episode with great apprehension and alarm, and so advised the Department of State. Afterward he reflected on the ironies of diplomatic history and paid a striking tribute to Davies by writing in his *Memoirs:*

Davies, with his brilliant, imaginative mind and his wide background of experience in China, was a rock of strength to us at that time in the Moscow embassy. I owe largely to him whatever insight I was able to muster in those years into the nature of Soviet policies toward the Far East. He was a man of broad, sophisticated, and skeptical political understanding, without an ounce of pro-Communist sympathies, and second to no one in his devotion to the interest of our government. To reflect that here, trying to bring some element of realism and sobriety into the view of General Hurley on the question of Soviet intentions, was a man who only shortly thereafter would have to suffer years of harassment and humiliation at the hands of congressional investigating committees and executive loyalty boards largely because of charges, inspired largely by this same General Hurley, to the effect that he was naive or pro-Communist in his sympathies—to realize this is to recognize the nightmarish quality of the world of fancy into which official Washington, and much of our public opinion, can be carried in those times when fear, anger, and emotionalism take over from reason in the conduct of our public life.[41]

The escalation of this kind of fear, anger, and emotionalism occurred in the wake of World War II, the subsequent struggle for power in China between the Communists and the Nationalists, and the bitter resignation of Hurley in 1945. Immediately upon resigning, Hurley charged that Davies and the other China Hands had sabotaged his efforts by siding with the Chinese Communists and vowed that he and his friends on the China Lobby would get revenge. When Davies returned to Washington to serve on the prestigious Policy Planning Staff, *Life* magazine was waiting with an article accusing him of being pro-Communist. Davies managed temporarily to avoid serious harm from this and other verbal attacks, but by 1949 his opponents arranged for his first review by a loyalty board. At this time he was cleared of all charges. But the accusations did not stop, and he continued to be investigated by the Department of State, the Senate Internal Security Subcommittee, and the Loyalty

Review Board. Indeed, by his own count, Davies was subjected to at least eight different probes questioning his loyalty to the United States. During this time, he found himself described as "one of the most potent influences in the Department furthering the cause of the Chinese Communists."[42]

When in the 1952 presidential campaign Dwight Eisenhower would not even defend his old friend General George Marshall against allegations of treason, Davies felt that there could be little hope for him. McCarthy, for one, continued to pressure for his scalp, shouting: "We still have John Paton Davies on the payroll" even though he was "part and parcel" of that "group which did so much toward delivering our Chinese friends into the Communist hands."[43] Faced with this kind of rhetoric, Davies and the Department of State believed it would be best to get as far out of the line of fire as possible. He therefore was sent as the deputy chief of mission to Lima, Peru. It proved to be his last assignment.

With the election of Eisenhower and the appointment of Dulles as Secretary of State, his Peruvian haven did not last for long. One of Dulles's first pronouncements regarding the Foreign Service was to announce that from then on, all career diplomats would have to demonstrate "positive loyalty" to whatever the new president and Congress might prescribe and that anything less than that would be "not tolerable at this time."[44] Dulles then invoked a new rule: No Foreign Service officer, no matter how often he might have passed loyalty or security tests in the past, could begin any assignment without first undergoing yet another clearance. To supervise this procedure, he hired a new security chief, Scott McLeod, a former newspaperman and administrative assistant to Senator Styles Bridges, a friend to the China Lobby. McLeod proved to be so objectionable that even his McCarthyite supporters eased him out after one year. But during his brief tenure, and under pressure from McCarthy and the China Lobby, McLeod decided that Davies should be reinvestigated.

Under McLeod's scrutiny, Davies once again found himself charged with having maintained close ties with the Chinese Communists during the war, writing reports based upon insufficient evidence, and having actively opposed and circumvented U.S. policy toward China. As a result of these charges, Dulles decided to set up yet another body to investigate Davies; this was the Security Hearing Board, headed by General Daniel Noce and composed of four others who knew little, if anything, about China or foreign affairs. They called General Hurley to testify, but refused to let anyone cross-examine him. In August 1954, the board indicated that it could find no concrete evidence of disloyalty, but nevertheless concluded that Davies be terminated for having "demonstrated a lack of judgment, discretion, and reliability."[45]

A copy of the unclassified sections of the board's report was sent to Davies at the American embassy in Peru. Once he read the charges against him, he decided to submit a thoughtful letter to General Noce, much of which appears in Davies's chapter in this book. In the letter he responded not only to the specific accusations made by the board but also to some of the larger questions about diplomacy, reporting events, and the ethics of speaking out rather than remaining silent. Dulles nevertheless remained unmoved by his arguments, called him in, and fired him.

The Journalists

The China Hands of the Foreign Service were not the only Americans reporting home on Chinese affairs. A number of distinguished journalists from the United States also had made China their "beat." These included such notables as Theodore White and Annalee Jacoby of *Time*, Arch Steel of the *Chicago Daily News*, Peggy and Tillman Durdin of the *New York Times*, Hugh Deane of the *Christian Science Monitor*, and John W. and Sylvia Powell of the *China Weekly Review*, among others. These journalists lived in China and came to know its people and politics, travel its countryside, appreciate its newsworthiness, establish contacts, and cultivate sources of information. Some, like Edgar Snow, learned the Chinese language, journeyed to secret Communist areas, interviewed Mao Tse-tung and Chou En-lai, and penetrated far beyond the scope of official contacts allowed by the Nationalists. In the process, many became the journalistic equivalents of the diplomatic China Hands—experts, that is, on Chinese affairs in their own right.

These journalists shared a number of important characteristics with their counterparts in diplomacy. They all knew China reasonably well and had invested much of their own lives and careers in this part of the world. They were all foreigners stationed in a country far from home and thus placed at both a literal and figurative distance from the sources of domestic power and influence that sometimes greatly affect diplomacy and journalism. Both groups tended, as Akira Iriye suggests, to be affected by the spirit of American political reformism, by a desire to support the underdog, and by the belief that technological progress and economic development could be matched by political institutions that would serve the rights and interests of all citizens. They also may have been inclined, as Ernest May argues, to believe that they knew the Chinese situation far better than their superiors back home and thus possessed great self-confidence when advocating a course of action or a change of policy that favored a particular outcome in China.

In addition, and of particular importance, the journalists, like their diplomatic colleagues, found themselves reporting information and making judgments that many in America absolutely did not want to hear. They bore witness to the same history the diplomats did: the Japanese invasion of Manchuria in 1931, the occupation of China six years later, the nature of Chiang Kai-shek's regime, the potential of Mao Tse-tung's Communist movement, the years of the United Front between the Nationalists and the Communists, American entry into World War II and its military efforts and frustrations in the Far East, the Chinese Civil War, and the emergence of the Cold War. They saw these many momentous events from the same location, through similar eyes, and reached similar conclusions, as Hood observes in Chapter 8. They became frustrated and angered by political leaders and editors who saw the world differently than they did, who did not share their opinions, and who had different agendas or faced particular kinds of political pressures.

For example, these reporters, like the diplomats, found themselves caught in an ethical dilemma between their professional responsibility to report the news truthfully as they saw it and their patriotic obligation to support an ally in the time of war. How could they explain that the early hopes of progressive reform in Chiang's government had materialized instead into a regime of repression and at the same time encourage Americans to support him? How could they report that Chiang's forces were militarily ineffective against the Japanese and that they secretly hoarded his supplies, if they were to foster the effort by the United States to provide even greater assistance during this time of need? How could they tell the members of the generally anti-Communist reading public in America that their Chinese Nationalist allies were corrupt while simultaneously reporting that the Chinese Communists were providing better government in their areas and were gaining increasing support throughout China? Or, how could they report the news and at the same time honor the restrictions of military and political censorship? The dilemmas in this situation became acute. White writes about his own experience in these bitter words: "I was in China, seeing this great revolution scream for simple reporting. But he [publisher Henry Luce] was in New York and felt it must be crushed. I *could* not yield from what I saw. He *would* not yield from how he saw it. I still insist, and know, that I was right and he was wrong in telling the story of China."[46] That story, however, was not told at the time. As correspondent Eric Sevareid also lamented about the Chinese situation: ". . . I had heard correctly. But it did not matter—I couldn't say it. . . . It was a condition of complete moral stalemate, and very little could be done about it."[47]

Given the problems and characteristics they shared, it is hardly surprising that American diplomats and journalists stationed in China sought each other out. Together they could speak in their own language in a foreign land, share information and compare notes, examine propositions and consider possibilities, recall the good times, try to discover the truth about events in China, and complain about their superiors at home and the local conditions at hand. They needed each other for both professional and personal reasons, and thus enjoyed each other's company. Those who participated in these discussions and gatherings still remember fondly to this day the special camaraderie and symbiotic relationship that they all shared.[48] Davies, for instance, refers in his chapter to the Press Hostel where all the journalists stayed as "the brightest spot" in Chungking and to the "amiable souls" within as those who "lightened the heart" in tense times.

These journalists and diplomats were also to share something else that none of them ever anticipated when they first filed their reports: charges of harming the interests of the United States government—charges that ranged from "poor judgment" and "disloyalty" to "sedition" and even "treason." Once the Chinese Communists emerged victorious in the civil war, forcing Chiang and his followers to flee to the island of Taiwan, and once the Korean War broke out and McCarthyism emerged as an important political force in America, the journalists who had written favorable reports about the Communists found themselves, like the China Hand diplomats, under enormous pressure. Theodore White, for example, to his great surprise and indignation, was suddenly confronted with charges that he had been one of those newspapermen who "lost China to the Reds."[49]

His collaborator on *Thunder Out of China*, Annalee Jacoby, was also subjected to public charges of being a "Communist" and a "Red" as Hood observes in his chapter. Many others shared a similar fate, with various degrees of intensity and suffering.

One of the most notable of these cases is that of John W. "Bill" Powell who recollects his ordeal in Chapter 7. He was born in Shanghai where his father, J. B. Powell, edited the *China Weekly Review*, a highly respected journal of news and opinion about Chinese affairs. The younger Powell came to the United States when one year old, returned to China at the age of five, and was evacuated when Chiang Kai-shek moved against the gates of Shanghai in the uprising of 1927.

Powell, as his father had, attended the Missouri School of Journalism. He returned again to China in 1940 and worked a stint for the Chinese-owned *China Press*. When the United States entered World War II, he joined the Office of War Information; he stayed in Washington and New York for a year and then was sent to Chungking where he worked with the press service and dropped leaflets for the United States out of army bombers over occupied Hong Kong and Canton.

After the war, Bill Powell took over the *China Weekly Review* from his father, who had suffered terribly in a Japanese prisoner camp. Less conservative than his father, who had seriously underestimated the Chinese Communists as "mere bandits,"[50] Bill tried to steer a middle course between them and Chiang's Nationalists. By broadening the paper's scope with articles by Chinese and American contributors, he rebuilt the journal's circulation. Bill then began to develop a sizable reputation as a journalist by expressing honest criticism of the corruption and maladministration in Chiang's government. In one notable case, he managed to pierce through the temporary news blackout over Taiwan, which was torn by revolt and virtually sealed off from the outside world, with an eyewitness account in 1947 of the deaths of at least 5,000 people in a massacre ordered by Chiang's authorities on the mainland.[51] After this story broke, the *Washington Post* referred to him as "a fearless news- paperman" and praised him as "one of the best-informed news- papermen on China conditions."[52]

These accolades and attention soon proved a mixed blessing. Bill Powell's criticism of Chiang's government quickly gave him an unofficial ranking as persona non grata among Nationalist leaders and their friends who accused him of "leftist tendencies."[53] When he remained in Shanghai after the Communists occupied the city in 1950 and continued to publish the *China Weekly Review,* the American editors of Luce's magazine *Time* regarded this as evidence of Communist sympathy. As they wrote in one article: "Old J. B., who called no man master, would have been surprised and shocked at its [the *China Weekly Review*] subservient tone. Son Bill had become an outright apologist for Communism."[54] After Bill's criticism of the Korean War, and his charges that the Americans had used germ warfare, *Newsweek* described his journal as "a Communist mouthpiece." It claimed that he had become "highly emotional where old J. B. had been realistic," developing "an unreasoning hatred of the Chinese regime and a correspondingly uncritical attitude toward the Communists." *Newsweek* went on to argue that his "leftward swing" had been accelerated by his 1947 marriage to Sylvia Campbell, an American formerly employed as a secretary to Madame Sun Yat-sen, "now a top Red." For all these reasons, the magazine labeled Powell as the "Red China Boy."[55]

Powell watched his journal go under in June of 1953 and left China for San Francisco with his wife and two children. Upon entry, his personal library was seized by customs on the grounds that its importation would be in violation of the Foreign Agents Registration Act. Slightly more than one year later, he received a summons to appear before the Senate Internal Security Subcommittee. Here, the thirty-five-year-old Powell heard himself described as a "murderer." A parade of former prisoners of war all testified that his *China Weekly Review* was "must" propaganda reading for indoctrination purposes in North Korean prison camps. They suggested that if the transports used to cart Powell's journal had been used instead for food and medical supplies, fewer American prisoners would have died. With such testimony before him, Republican Senator William

E. Jenner declared that he would ask the Justice Department to press treason charges against him.[56] Hearings before the subcommittee continued for both Sylvia and Bill Powell. Under a constant barrage of questions, she replied on one occasion, "I am an American . . . I have never done anything I would apologize or be sorry for."[57] The accusations alone, however, were enough to cause her to be fired from her job. One time when Bill could not be found, Republican Senator Herman Welker declared that "John W. Powell is today roaming the country free to continue his vicious propaganda in behalf of Communist China."[58] One witness went so far as to assert that Powell "made Benedict Arnold look like an amateur."[59] In one published report, the subcommittee asserted: "There is no precedent in recent American history—if, indeed, there is a precedent in all American history—for the conduct of John W. Powell. His unspeakable betrayal of America's cause in the Far East is matched only by his arrogance toward the Senate of the United States."[60]

Powell's career, reputation, and life went from bad to worse during 1956 when he was indicted by a federal grand jury on twelve counts of sedition. They were handed down after what was described as a secret and "highly urgent" session.[61] The indictments charged him with attempting to cause "insubordination, disloyalty, and refusal of duty in the military and naval forces of the United States" through the issues of his journal; willfully publishing false statements; and engaging in "activities designed to interfere with the operation and success of the military forces of the United States and to promote the success of its enemies" during the Korean War.[62] Powell responded by denying the charges and declared: "It's an attempt to shut me up and stop debate on our China policy which is bankrupt. Things have happened in China—which we may not approve of—but they've happened and we can't go on pretending [they did not occur]."[63] He repeated that he was simply telling the truth in his reports about Chiang's corruption and America's mistaken foreign policy toward Asia. "Our policy doesn't recognize the revolution as an accomplished fact," he said, "and by not recognizing it, we are flying in the face of history."[64]

The 1958 trial of Bill and Sylvia Powell ended in a mistrial. The U.S. attorney then submitted a new charge of treason against them for allegedly giving aid and comfort to the Chinese Communist enemies. The charge of treason carried a minimum penalty of five years in prison or a $10,000 fine and a maximum penalty of death. Viewing the lack of evidence and the failure of the government to produce the witnesses required by law, the grand jury refused to indict and this serious charge was dropped. The sedition charges still hung over their heads, however, for several more years. Indeed, the Powells lived under the uncertainty of indictments and public pressure against them until 1961 when the charges were finally dropped by the Department of Justice. Those years took a heavy toll; they were forced to borrow money from family and friends for legal fees and occasionally send their children away. They lost their jobs, had their telephones tapped by the Federal Bureau of Investigation, and, in effect, were blackballed as professional journalists.[65]

Powell's fate, it must be remembered, was hardly unique. Numerous other journalists also lost their jobs merely because of accusations about pro-Communist sympathies.[66] Those who invoked the First Amendment's freedom of speech or the Fifth Amendment's protection against self-incrimination found their statements interpreted as prima facie evidence of guilt. In this process they were shocked to discover that the accusations came not only from individual politicians like Joseph McCarthy, Patrick McCarran, William Jenner, Herman Welker, and other members of the Senate Internal Security Subcommittee or the House Committee on Un-American Activities but also from some of their own colleagues in journalism. Editors and columnists from the *Los Angeles Examiner* and the *San Francisco Examiner* of the Hearst chain, the *Chicago Tribune*, and the *New York Daily News*, among others, competed with each other to reveal presumed spies in their ranks, to purge fellow travelers, and to selectively present the news. Henry Luce of *Time-Life* possessed very definite ideas of what should—and should not—be reported about Chiang Kai-shek and made sure that his publications conformed. The *New York Times* refused for several years to publish a single book review on China written by any Chinese specialist associated with the Institute of Pacific Relations, an organization once accused of being "the center of all Communist activity in the Far Eastern field."[67]

In the end, of course, the senators censured their colleague Joseph McCarthy. The country ceased its campaign of hate, unsupported accusations, and suspicions. Moreover, in the end, the China Hands had their security clearances restored and at least some of the reporters found employment in the field of journalism. But this occurred only after many careers and reputations were ruined. In the process, the United States thus lost many of its most knowledgeable and courageous experts on China. Whether the elimination of this valuable expertise poked out "the eyes and ears of the State Department on Asian affairs" and blinded American foreign policy, as White argues,[68] thereby leading the United States into both the Korean War and Vietnam War, sparks continuous debate, as the chapters by Melby and May make clear. But the fact remains that America did fight two major wars in Asia during the postwar years and suffered through more than twenty years of intense hostility with the People's Republic of China.

The long and bitter freeze in Sino-American relations was not broken until President Richard Nixon made his historic trip to China in 1972. The former congressman who had so actively engaged in the anticommunism battle of the McCarthy era by this time had recognized the necessity for communicating with China, as had the Chinese in realizing the importance of discussions with America. In his Peking speech, Nixon stressed the common interests that transcended the ideological gulf, actually quoted the writings of Mao Tse-tung, and announced: "There is no reason for us to be enemies."[69] His sentiments were repeated when Republican presidents Gerald Ford and Ronald Reagan also visited the Chinese Communists. Ironically, by 1986, conditions and attitudes on both sides had changed so much that *Time,* which had done so much to distort America's image of China during World War II, actually named Mao's successor of the People's Republic of China, Deng Xiaoping, as its Man of the Year for an unprecedented second time.[70] These dramatic changes suggest that perhaps after all this time, the China Hands finally have been vindicated. They also bring to mind Eric Sevareid's observation about the fate of the China Hands. "It is rather extraordinary," he wrote, "how men must plot and combine and negotiate merely to tell the truth. It always comes out somewhere, some time. But sometimes it comes too late."[71]

Notes

1. Joseph McCarthy, as cited in United States, Congress, Senate, Committee on Foreign Relations, Report No. 2108, *State Department*

Employee Loyalty Investigation (Washington, D.C.: Government Printing Office, 1950), p. 2.

2. See David Caute, *The Great Fear: The Anti-Communist Purge Under Truman and Eisenhower* (New York: Simon and Schuster, 1978), p. 310.

3. John King Fairbank, *The United States and China* (New York: Viking, 1958 ed.), p. 261.

4. Theodore White, *In Search of History: A Personal Adventure* (New York: Harper & Row, 1978), p. 132. Also see Barbara Tuchman, *Stilwell and the American Experience in China 1911–1945* (New York: Macmillan, 1971).

5. Joseph Stilwell, as cited in White, *In Search of History*, p. 134.

6. Ibid., p. 136.

7. See Joseph Keeley, *The China Lobby Man: The Story of Alfred Kohlberg* (New Rochelle: Arlington House, 1969); Ross Koen, *The China Lobby in American Politics* (New York: Harper & Row, 1974); Malcolm Hobbs, "Chiang's Washington Front," *Nation* (24 December 1949):619–620; and for the later period, Stanley Bachrack, *The Committee of One Million: The China Lobby in American Politics, 1953–71* (New York: Columbia University Press, 1976).

8. White, *In Search of History*, p. 76.

9. Ibid., p. 74.

10. See David Barrett, *Dixie Mission: The United States Army Observer Group in Yenan, 1944* (Berkeley: Center for Chinese Studies, 1970).

11. Chiang Kai-shek, as cited in E. J. Kahn, *The China Hands: America's Foreign Service Officers and What Befell Them* (New York: Viking, 1975), p. 127.

12. See Donald Lohbeck, *Patrick J. Hurley* (Chicago: Regnery, 1956).

13. See White, *In Search of History*, pp. 197–198; Kahn, *The China Hands*, p. 123n; and Russell Buhite, *Patrick J. Hurley and American Foreign Policy* (Ithaca: Cornell University Press, 1973).

14. See the letter from Theodore White to Henry Luce and David Hulburd, 29 November 1944, a copy of which is on file in the Mansfield Papers, Series XIX: Personal, Container No. 511, located in the University of Montana Archives. This matter is treated particularly well in Charles Hood's dissertation, "'China Mike' Mansfield" (Pullman: Washington State University, 1980), pp. 286ff.

15. Mike Mansfield's confidential China Mission Report to Roosevelt, dated 3 January 1945, was printed later in U.S. Department of State, *Foreign Relations of the United States* [hereafter cited as *FRUS*], *1945*, Vol. VII, *The Far East: China* (Washington, D.C.: Government Printing Office, 1969). This quotation can be found on p. 8. Mansfield's milder,

and public, report can be found in "China Mission Reports," in the Mansfield Papers, Series XIX: Personal, Container No. 510.

16. Ibid., pp. 2–26.

17. Mansfield letter to Edward R. Stettinius, 16 January 1945, "China Mission Folders," in the Mansfield Papers, Series XIX: Personal, Container No. 511.

18. See U.S. Department of State, *FRUS, 1944*, Vol. VI, *China* (Washington, D.C.: Government Printing Office, 1967), pp. 674ff.

19. Eric Sevareid, *Not So Wild a Dream* (New York: Knopf, 1946), p. 352.

20. See Kahn, *The China Hands*, p. 145; and Davies's Chapter 2.

21. Patrick Hurley to Harry Truman, 26 November 1945, in *FRUS, 1945*, Vol. VII: 722–726.

22. See the discussion in Nancy Tucker, "Nationalist China's Decline," in Dorothy Borg and Waldo Heinricks, eds., *Uncertain Years: Chinese-American Relations, 1947–1950* (New York: Columbia University Press, 1980), pp. 131–171.

23. The words are those of Caute, *The Great Fear*, p. 303.

24. Senate, Report No. 2108, p. 15.

25. Ibid.; and Caute, *The Great Fear*, p. 304. For a different perspective, see William F. Buckley, Jr., and Brent Bozell, *McCarthy and His Enemies* (Chicago: Regnery, 1954).

26. U.S. Department of State, *United States Relations with China, with Special Reference to the Period 1944–1949* (Washington, D.C.: Government Printing Office, 1949), pp. xv–xvi. Also see Lyman P. Van Slyke, ed., *The China White Paper, August 1949* (Stanford: Stanford University Press, 1967).

27. Joseph McCarthy, as cited in Senate, Report No. 2108, p. 2.

28. Clarence Gauss, as cited in Kahn, *The China Hands*, p. 65.

29. George Kennan, as cited in John Paton Davies, *Dragon by the Tail* (New York: Norton, 1972), p. 319.

30. See John Service, *Lost Chance in China: The World War II Despatches of John S. Service*, Joseph Esherick, ed., (New York: Random House, 1974), pp. 161ff. For his most recent commentary about the experience, see John Service, "Changes in China, New and Not New," *US-China Review* (July-August 1985):6–10.

31. Patrick J. Hurley, as cited in Service, *Lost Chance in China*, p. 358.

32. His own account of this case can be found in John Service, *The Amerasia Papers: Some Problems in the History of US-China Relations* (Berkeley: University of California Press, 1971).

33. Alfred Kohlberg, as cited in Kahn, *The China Hands*, p. 50.

34. Styles Bridges, as cited in ibid., p. 192.

35. Hiram Bingham, chairman of the Loyalty Review Board, letter of 12 December 1952, as reproduced in "The Meaning of the Ruling in the Vincent Case," *Foreign Service Journal* (January 1953):17. Also see the recent discussion in Gary May, *China Scapegoat: The Diplomatic Ordeal of John Carter Vincent* (Washington, D.C.: New Republic Books, 1979).

36. Sevareid, *Not So Wild a Dream*, p. 292.

37. Sevareid, CBS radio broadcast of 8 November 1954, as cited in Kahn, *The China Hands*, p. 30.

38. Davies, *Dragon by the Tail*, between pp. 224–225.

39. See *FRUS, 1944*, Vol. VI, *China*, pp. 667ff.; and ibid., pp. 361–363.

40. Albert Wedemeyer, *Wedemeyer Reports!* (New York: Holt, 1958), p. 319.

41. George Kennan, *Memoirs, 1925–1950* (Boston: Little, Brown, 1967), p. 239.

42. See Kahn, *The China Hands*, p. 59.

43. Joseph McCarthy, as cited in "John P. Davies," *Foreign Service Journal* (May 1954):48.

44. See the excellent discussion of this process in Kahn, *The China Hands*, p. 247.

45. "Documents in the John Paton Davies, Jr., Case," *Foreign Service Journal* (December 1954):44 and 46.

46. White, *In Search of History*, p. 210.

47. Sevareid, *Not So Wild a Dream*, pp. 317–318.

48. See most recently, James C. Thomson, Jr., "China Reporting Revisited," *Nieman Reports*, XXXVII (Spring 1983):30–34.

49. White, *In Search of History*, p. 201.

50. "J.B.'s Boy," *Time*, 24 March 1947.

51. "U.S. Editor Charges Chiang Troops Butchered 5,000 Formosa Rebels," *San Francisco Chronicle*, 31 March 1947.

52. "China Editor's Son Has Own Rapier Pen," *Washington Post*, 6 July 1947.

53. Ibid.

54. "Dream Street, Shanghai," *Time*, 17 July 1950.

55. "Red China Boy," *Newsweek*, 11 October 1954.

56. Ibid.

57. "S.F. Wife Defies Red Probe," *San Francisco Call-Bulletin*, 13 December 1954.

58. Ibid.

59. Cited in "Got $10,000?" *San Francisco News*, 26 April 1956.

60. Senate Internal Security Subcommittee, as cited in "S.F. Jury Indicts Writer—Sedition," *San Francisco Chronicle*, 26 April 1956.

61. Ibid.

62. Ibid.

63. "Got $10,000?" *San Francisco News*, 26 April 1956.

64. "Powell Defends His Writings," *San Francisco Chronicle*, 26 April 1956.

65. The story is presented in "Germ Warfare Charges," *San Francisco Sunday Examiner and Chronicle*, 13 March 1977.

66. See James Aronson, *The Press and the Cold War* (Indianapolis: Bobbs-Merrill, 1970); James Wechsler, *Reflections of an Angry Middle-Aged Editor* (New York: Random House, 1960); and Alan Barth, *Government by Investigation* (New York: Viking, 1955).

67. Caute, *The Great Fear*, pp. 316 and 448.

68. White, *In Search of History*, p. 395.

69. Richard Nixon, as cited in Henry Kissinger, *White House Years* (Boston: Little, Brown, 1979), p. 1070.

70. "China," *Time*, 6 January 1986.

71. Sevareid, *Not So Wild a Dream*, p. 352.

JOHN PATON DAVIES

2
The China Hands In Practice: The Personal Experience

The term "China Hand" as used in my salad days in Peking, Mukden, and Hankow, was preceded by the adjective old—"Old China Hand." The Old China Hand was, typically, a prosperous British or American merchant, long resident in Shanghai or some other treaty port, who looked down on the Chinese and was ignorant of their language, whose leisure time was spent in sport at a club exclusively for foreigners, and who was well preserved: gin before sundown and scotch thereafter.

The abbreviated term "China Hand," I gather, is currently used to denote particularly those of us who served the American government in China before and during World War II, who fraternized with Chinese and studied their language, whose idea of fun was to explore remote reaches of the Middle Kingdom, and who were in many cases, from 1944 on, ill preserved: denounced and defamed. The personal experiences of these China Hands in the line of duty raise many different kinds of issues and pose a variety of questions. As opinions among the China Hands varied, however, it would be well to avoid thinking of us all as somehow of one mind. I do not pretend to speak for any of my former colleagues. The point of view that follows, therefore, is mine.

Those of us in the Foreign Service who specialized in China normally underwent two years of initiation in Chinese language, history, and economics at our embassy in Peking. The armed services assigned a few officers for similar study. In addition to China specialization, the Department of State supported language studies for Foreign Service officers in Russian, Japanese, and Arabic. The graduates of Russian studies during the early years of the Roosevelt sway were given a hard time because FDR regarded them as anti-Soviet. The Japan specialists were, in the late thirties and early forties, often accused of being apologists for Tokyo's aggressions. In much the same way, the Foreign Service Arabists are now and have been since 1948 stigmatized as enemies of Israel. So, area specialization in the Foreign Service has not always been rewarded with deafening applause.

After my tour in Peking, my career took me to Mukden, Manchuria, as vice consul. Here the American consulate served as an important listening post in what was historically an area of international conflict among China, Japan, and Russia. In 1938 I was assigned to Hankow, under seige and then occupation by the invading Japanese army. After this assignment, the Department of State called me back to Washington to the Far Eastern Division. I was vacationing when the Pearl Harbor attack occurred on December 7, 1941. Returning to the office, found the Far Eastern Division terribly distraught over its failure to forewarn. It was also evident after this surprise that the Department of State quickly would become a backwater. Military considerations and strategic policy now would dominate government.

Shortly after Christmas, I dined with Major General Joseph W. Stilwell and Colonel Frank Dorn. I had first met them both in Peking, and they were experienced in Chinese affairs. The general and Dorn now were preparing to go overseas. It was later revealed that Stilwell had been designated to command a Northwest African landing. Eager to get away from my State Department desk and off to war, I asked Dorn if he could persuade the former military attaché to an ambassador to take me along as an innovation—a diplomatic attaché to a general. Some days later Dorn told me that Stilwell had arranged for the War Department to ask State to assign me to his staff.

Meanwhile, the plans for a Northwest African operation appeared to me, at best, premature. The chief of staff, General George C. Marshall, then persuaded Stilwell to accept a hydra-headed, disembodied appointment as chief of a nonexistent Allied Staff to Generalissimo Chiang Kai-shek and commanding general of the scant, skeletal American forces in China-Burma-India. Stilwell was also designated commander of the unenthusiastic Chinese expeditionary forces in Burma, sent to bolster the demoralized, hodgepodge, British-Indian-Gurkha-Burmese defenders of that colony.

On February 10, 1942, my department designated me a second secretary of our embassy at Chungking but detailed me to General Stilwell's Mission. So, instead of plunging into Africa, I found myself back in China—and in Burma and India. Such are the usages of fate.

Because the Japanese controlled the western Pacific and coastal China at that time, our route went eastward across the Atlantic and central Africa through India and northern Burma to China's mountainous backdoor, Yunnan province. Stilwell was in Burma when I caught up with him in March 1942. He was nominally and profanely in command of nine Chinese divisions skittishly resisting the implacable Japanese offensive. Stilwell found it difficult to talk with the Generalissimo, who enraged him by issuing from Chungking scatterbrained operational orders behind the American general's back to Chinese officers as far down as the regimental level. With reference to working with me, the general said, "There's nothing I can tell you about how to run your job. You're a free agent. All you have to do is to keep things running smoothly between the civil authorities here and us." Those were my orders—nothing in writing then or thereafter.

With the defense of Burma and the civil authorities crumbling like a sand castle washed by the surge of an incoming tide, there was nothing constructive that I could do in Burma. I accompanied Stilwell to Chungking. There I called on the ambassador, Clarence E. Gauss. The ambassador, like Stilwell, was strong-willed, a China Hand, governed by the Puritan ethic and professionally accomplished. Gauss had the same opinion as my superiors in the Far Eastern Division about my detail to Stilwell—that it was essentially frivolous. I should be put back to work at an embassy desk. Some months later, according to Stilwell, Gauss told the general that he wanted me back at the embassy. To this Stilwell replied in his less-than-ingratiating manner that the ambassador did not have a prayer.

In calculating where I could be most useful to Stilwell, I decided India, about which we were astonishingly ignorant. It was the essential base from which to supply China. Furthermore, with the rapid northward advance of the Japanese in Burma and the appearance of a Japanese naval task force freely roaming the Bay of Bengal, India appeared to be in imminent peril. Not only were the military defenses of India weak and most of the population lacking will to fight, but Gandhi was preparing to launch a campaign of mass nonviolent noncooperation against the British and, should the Japanese invade, was planning to use this as the only form of resistance to be used against the new conquerors.

For much of the rest of 1942 I traveled in India, interviewing Nehru, Gandhi, Jinnah, and other leaders of the Congress party, the Muslim League, Hindu Mahasabha, and the Untouchables. I also talked with British officials, Indian princes, industrialists, intellectuals, and a pungent variety of persons on trains, provincial buses, and a launch plying the lotus canals of Travancore. My memoranda of significant conversations and a concluding report on the extraordinarily complex and febrile situation in India went to Stilwell, our mission at New Delhi, and the State Department. I concluded that unless the British raj could arrange for an orderly transfer of authority to an Indian successor government or governments by the end of the war, the subcontinent was probably doomed to a time of frightful trouble. The prime issue in India, and in former European possessions in Southeast Asia, was colonialism. There could be no return to the pre-December 7, 1941, status quo. The U.S. government should guard against being drawn into any attempt by our allies to retain or reimpose colonial rule.

This account of a China Hand in India is a digression with a purpose. The American envoy in India, William Phillips (a true New England gentleman of the old school), and those in the State Department dealing with Indian affairs supported and commended my activities and reports on the subcontinent. The British, who did not appreciate at all my criticism of their colonial rule nor my suggestion that Washington should press them to transfer authority to the Indians, nevertheless treated me with civility rather than character assassination. I say all of this as a point of reference against which to measure the treatment of the China Hands from late 1944 onward.

If the prime issue in India and Southeast Asia was colonialism, then that for the Chinese was the expected civil war between the National government and the Communists following an American defeat of Japan. Intimations of this emerged in my conversations with Chinese on my first visit to Chungking. On successive visits I sensed a growing concern, for Communist strength was steadily expanding behind the Japanese lines. My first survey of government-Communist relations was in June 1943. In my report to Stilwell I said,

The Kuomintang (the Nationalists' political party) and Chiang Kai-shek recognize that the Communists, with the popular support which they enjoy and their reputation for administrative reform and honesty, represent a challenge to the Central Government and its spoils system. The Generalissimo cannot admit the seemingly innocent demands of the Communists that their party be legalized and democratic processes be put into practice. To do so would probably mean the abdication of the Kuomintang and the provincial satraps.

The Communists, on the other hand, dare not accept the Central Government's invitation that they disband their armies and be absorbed in the national body politic. To do so would be to invite extinction.

This impasse will probably be resolved, American and other foreign observers in Chungking agree, by an attempt by the Central Government to liquidate the Communists. This action may be expected to precipitate a civil war from which one of the two contending factions will emerge dominant. . . .

It would only be natural that, should Chiang attack the Communists, the latter would turn for aid to their immediate neighbor, the Soviet Union. And as such an attack would probably not be launched until after the defeat of Japan, the Communists might expect with good reason to receive Russian aid. . . .

A Central Government attack would therefore in all probability force the Communists into the willing arms of the Russians. The position of the political doctrinaires who have been subservient to Moscow would be strengthened by such an attack. The present trend of the Chinese Communists toward more or less democratic nationalism—confirmed in six years of fighting for the Chinese motherland—would thereby be reversed and they could be expected to retrogress to the position of a Russian satellite.

I continued my analysis of this situation with the following words:

In these circumstances they would not be a weak satellite. With
Russian arms, with Russian technical assistance, and with the
popular appeal which they have, the Chinese Communists might
be expected to defeat the Central Government and eventually to
take over the control of most if not all of China. It may be assumed
that a Russo-Chinese bloc, with China as a subservient member
of the partnership, would not be welcomed by us. The effect of
such a bloc upon the rest of Asia and upon world stability would
be undesirable. . . . Chiang and his Central Government recognize
that they cannot defeat the Communists and the Soviet Union
without foreign aid. Such aid would naturally be sought from the
United States and possibly Britain. . . .

In these circumstances we may anticipate that Chiang Kai-shek
will exert every effort and resort to every strategem to involve us
in active support of the Central Government. We will probably be
told that if fresh American aid is not forthcoming all of China and
eventually all of Asia will be swept by communism [which, it should
be added, is now what we are being told about Central America].
It will be difficult for us to resist such appeals, especially in view
of our moral commitments to continued assistance to China during
the post-war period.

It is therefore not inconceivable that, should Chiang attempt to
liquidate the Communists, we would find ourselves entangled not
only in a civil war in China but also drawn into conflict with the
Soviet Union.

I concluded this survey with a plea that the president ask Chiang
Kai-shek to allow the establishment of an American consulate or
military observers' group in Communist-held territory. Chou had said
that American representation at Yenan, the Communist "capital,"
would be welcome.

It is evident now that in this prognosis, more than two years
before the civil war erupted, I underestimated the Communists'
potential for rapid growth, as I overestimated the degree to which
the Soviet Union was willing or needed to intervene on behalf of
its Chinese proselytes. Nor did I predict that the Communists' military
victories would be to a considerable extent won with American
weapons taken from the Nationalists.

The brightest spot in Chunking was the Press Hostel, where the
foreign correspondents were penned. It was not the premises but

those within it that lightened the heart. Here were to be found at various times: Arch Steele, Theodore H. White, Brooks Atkinson, Tillman Durdin, Eric Sevareid, Edgar Snow, and other amiable souls. Again, this was a symbiotic relationship between the press and members of the diplomatic corps, out of which I derived more benefit than I gave.

Chou En-lai headed the Communist office in Chungking. I met with him occasionally, sometimes for a meal at a restaurant. Any vacant table near us was quickly occupied by neatly dressed men who listened silently from their stools in our direction, thereby provoking Chou's mirth. I assumed that agents of Tai Li, Chiang's secret police boss, reported to their headquarters my meetings with any of the Communists. Years later I learned that Nationalist intelligence operatives also wrote and passed on to our State Department's excitable security officials reports of juicy rendezvous between Communists and me that did not and could not have occurred because I was hundreds or thousands of miles away.

Miffed that Washington gave China lower priority than the war against Hitler and the Pacific campaigns, Chiang pressed Roosevelt to send his top troubleshooter, Harry Hopkins, to Chungking for consultations. Instead, in July 1942, another presidential assistant, Lauchlin Currie, was dispatched to placate the Generalissimo. Stilwell asked me to make myself helpful to Currie and to sniff out what the White House emissary was up to. Neither the general nor the ambassador was informed by Washington or by Currie what was going on. This was a typical situation at Chungking with self-important visitors.

Although he was chummy with me, Currie confided nothing, neither in Chungking nor when I accompanied him back to Washington. After my return to India I learned that Currie had recommended Stilwell's recall. It later appeared that he also recommended the removal of Gauss and T. V. Soong, who was foreign minister and Madame Chiang's clever and brash brother. None of Currie's recommendations was acted upon.

The Generalissimo and his wife in all probability were behind Currie's presumptuous move against Stilwell. The American general's compulsions to combat drove him into a confrontation with Chiang. As I reported to the ambassador in March 1943:

Acutely aware of their relative military exhaustion, of the fact that they can be no stronger politically than they are militarily, of the importance of appearing as powerful as possible at the peace table and of the likelihood of civil war with the Chinese Communists after the peace, the Chinese government is, not surprisingly, pursuing a policy of conservation of military strength. . . .

We recognized before December 7, 1941 that China was endeavoring to get us to fight its battle against Japan. . . .

China's policy, now that we are fighting the Japanese, is to remain technically in the war so as to be able to sit at the peace table as a "fighting" ally, to expend as little as possible of its strength and to rely upon . . . primarily the United States—to defeat Japan.

So from the Burma campaign until he finally rid himself of the gadfly American general, Chiang Kai-shek urged transient Washington personages visiting Chungking to arrange for Stilwell's removal. Roosevelt's initial inclinations to accede to Chiang's importunities were overcome by General Marshall and Secretary of War Henry Stimson.

In 1942, 1943, and 1944 Stilwell sent me on visits to Washington. My function was to offset as far as I could, through briefing newsmen and other influential persons, the anti-Stilwell propaganda fomented by the Chiangs and their Washington lobby. The Chiangs not only wanted Stilwell removed, but his replacement to be General Claire Chennault, who commanded, under Stilwell, the XIV Air Force. Chennault's extravagant claims that, given air reinforcement, he could cripple Japan by air action endeared him to the Chiangs, for this would obviate the need for doing what Stilwell insisted on: reforming the Chinese Army and committing it to the offensive.

Chennault's aide was Captain Joseph Alsop, in peacetime a newspaper columnist. Alsop was an ardent Chennault partisan and later also an enthusiastic confederate of T. V. Soong, the foreign minister who sought to oust Stilwell. Alsop had wide contacts in Washington, including Hopkins in the White House, which he vigorously cultivated. I mention these intrigues to provide a glimpse of the labyrinthine maneuvering in what may be blithely referred to as the Sino-American war effort.

Stilwell took me with him to the November 1943 Roosevelt-Churchill-Chiang conference near Cairo. We met with Hopkins and then with the president and Hopkins together. In a characteristically discursive and vague Rooseveltian conversation, two statements interested me. In reply to my question about what we should do if the Chiang regime disintegrated, Roosevelt immediately replied, without any qualification, that we should bolster the next in line. Then Hopkins made the point, once to Stilwell and me, and again to FDR, that a small closely knit group was needed to run American foreign affairs and by implication included the general and me in it. We did not take the suggestion seriously. I did, however, comply later with Hopkins's request that I send him copies of significant reports of mine.

The Generalissimo finally acceded in 1944 to American pressure for stationing an American observers group at Yenan, the Communist capital. The group was headed by a China Hand, Colonel David D. Barrett, who was, by experience, understanding, and tact, an ideal choice. Because of our detail to Stilwell it was possible to include in the military group at various times colleagues also detailed to Stilwell—John S. Service, Raymond P. Ludden, John K. Emmerson, and my wife and I.

The setting was extraordinary—assorted American military and diplomatic officers housed, fed, and entertained by a revolutionary hierarchy that was readily accessible for discussion on almost any topic. We were thus able to view the future rulers of China close-up.

Out of these contacts, the indefatigable Service was enabled to write a series of brilliant, historically significant reports on the Chinese Communists. Ludden, under the protection of relays of Communist troops and guerrillas, penetrated deep behind the Japanese lines to observe firsthand the impressive extent of Communist control and popular support in nominally occupied territory. Emmerson was introduced to and interviewed at revealing length a Japanese Communist leader heading the indoctrination of docile Japanese prisoners of war. And I concluded, and so reported, that China's destiny was not Chiang's but the Communists'.

Following Currie, Republican presidential candidate Wendell Willkie, and Vice President Wallace, Patrick J. Hurley was the last of the itinerant Pooh-Bahs to be inflicted upon Stilwell and Gauss. Hurley was a Republican lawyer, a reserve major general, and a former secretary of war. Everyone—Marshall, Stimson, Roosevelt, and Stilwell—thought at the outset that Hurley's assignment to harmonize relations between Chiang and Stilwell was a good idea. So did I. That he failed in this mission was excusable. But then he went on in blind conceit committing himself—and his government—to harmonizing Chiang and the Communists. That eventually ended in another and even more humiliating fiasco.

The high-noon showdown between Chiang and Stilwell was precipitated by a demand Roosevelt made on the Generalissimo. Exasperated by more than two years of petulance and stalling on the part of Chiang, Marshall unwisely obtained Roosevelt's concurrence in a message to the Generalissimo demanding that he "at once" place "General Stilwell in unrestricted command of all your forces." This was obviously unacceptable to the Generalissimo. Hurley could not reconcile the deadlock. It was broken by Stilwell's recall in mid-October 1944.

With an expansive Hurley assuming the airs of an American viceroy, the weary Gauss resigned. For my part, I thought it was time to get in a position to watch the end of the Pacific War and the beginning of the Chinese Civil War from Moscow. I therefore wrote a personal letter to Charles E. Bohlen, the ranking Russian specialist at the department, asking if he would arrange for my transfer to the embassy at Moscow. I planned to function in the meantime under Stilwell's successor, General Albert C. Wedemeyer, in the same capacity as I had under Stilwell.

Reconciliation between Chiang and the Communists, and thus the unification of China, was a mandate Hurley imposed upon himself. His approach to the problem was both uninformed and deluded. He assumed that bringing the two sides together was rather like creating a wartime bipartisanship in the United States. (He said at one time that the Communists were like Republicans only they had arms!) I was in Yenan when he first arrived there and uttered his Choctaw war whoop, to the bewilderment of the assembled Marxists. At the first opportunity for private conversation, I warned him that the Communists would be tough to bargain with and that he should not expect that they would yield to terms acceptable to Chiang. This did not please Hurley, who pointedly suggested that I return to Chungking by the next day's headquarters' plane. I did so.

In November 1944 Hurley had taken a proposal cleared by Chiang to Yenan calling for military unification under Chiang and, among other things, "the establishment in China of a government of the people, for the people, and by the people." The Communists inveigled him into changing the proposal to provide for a revision of the National government into a coalition and to include other clauses unacceptable to the Generalissimo. Not to be outdone, Hurley simply threw in provisions embracing the Bill of Rights, the Four Freedoms, and as a bonus, freedom of conscience. The Communists were enchanted, for Chiang could not accept such license and they would win a public relations victory. As a stamp of approval, Hurley signed copies of the Communists' counterproposal and took one back to Soong.

The agitated foreign minister told Hurley that the Communists had sold him a bill of goods and that the government would never grant what Yenan had requested. Hurley asserted to me that the Communist proposals were eminently fair and if the negotiations broke down it would be the government's fault. He attributed the government's rejection to sabotage by Soong, whom he characterized as a "crook," for he could not bring himself to admit that the Generalissimo would turn down the Yenan proposals that he had signed and brought to Chungking. In the same way that he had resented my warning at Yenan, he reacted with quick, suspicious hostility to anyone who spoke a well-meaning word of caution to him—be it *Time* correspondent Theodore White or the British ambassador.

The mercurial Hurley confided in me from time to time and even invited me to live with him in the official residence once his appointment as ambassador became effective. As he was above reporting normally to the department and kept the embassy staff in the dark, I wrote personal letters to the chief of the China Division reporting what I knew of the negotiations.

By December 1944, Hurley was thoroughly entangled in the Chungking-Yenan intrigue. T. V. Soong manipulated Hurley's need to find a scapegoat for his inability to unify China. Soong urged him to remove me from China, charging that I was conniving with the Communists to thwart his efforts. On December 15, Hurley told me for a second time that Soong was pressing him to replace me with Alsop, adding "T. V. figures that you know too much; he wants to set up his own pipeline to me."

Meanwhile, I continued reporting as I had under Stilwell. In sum, I saw Chiang's strength declining relative to that of the Communists. I doubted that Hurley could bring about a reconciliation between the two sides, especially after he insisted that Yenan accept the Generalissimo's supremacy in a coalition. We had to face up to an oncoming civil war. Unless we established relations with the Communists, which Yenan definitely wanted, the Communists would go by default to Moscow. Thus, the Communists would win the civil war, but they would become dependent on the Soviet Union and be drawn into the Soviet orbit. This would tilt the balance of power in East Asia against us.

From Bohlen came word that Averell Harriman, our ambassador to the Soviet Union, was expecting me. It was with scant regret that I left Chungking in January 1945.

At Moscow I was behind an embassy desk again, working for an ambassador with clout at the White House and for his deputy, George Kennan, one of the most illuminative minds I have encountered. The embassy atmosphere was orderly and creative—most refreshing.

Then Hurley blew in. He had left his post at Chungking with a plan to line up Roosevelt, Churchill, and Stalin in support of Chiang's supremacy in a coalition government. With this heavy artillery, he would bring Yenan into line under the Generalissimo. His first stop was Washington, where he claimed to obtain the support of a wasted Roosevelt, only a few weeks from death. Then he saw Churchill and received an indifferent concurrence from the British. Next, Stalin sounded as if he was in agreement with Hurley. Kennan and I drafted a message to the State Department cautioning that Stalin's words could mean all things to all people. And in any event, unification depended on conditions acceptable to Yenan. Hurley's fundamental error was underestimation of the Communists. They were not amenable to dictation from anyone—even Stalin.

Returning to Chungking, Hurley evicted the principal China Hands, muzzled the rest of his staff, and prohibited reporting critical of the government. He made no progress in his negotiations.

World War II came to an end in August 1945. Immediately the two sides in China began jockeying for position. The civil war had begun, whereupon the American government, shedding any pretense of impartiality, intervened on the side of the Nationalists. Hurley's presumptuous schemes for unifying China were dashed.

He left China and in an erratic performance at Washington, resigned on November 27. "The professional Foreign Service men," Hurley told the press, "sided with the Chinese Communists armed party." He also charged that we advised the Communists that his efforts in preventing the collapse of the National government did not represent American policy and that we advised the Communists to decline unification of their forces with the National army unless they were given control. In addition to uttering these falsehoods, Hurley testified to the Senate Foreign Relations Committee that Service, three other China Hands, and I were the ones that he deemed culpable. The State Department asked me to comment on the Hurley charges. I replied, from Moscow, that they were false.

In 1947 I was transferred to the Policy Planning Staff of the Department of State, headed by George Kennan. I was welcomed by John Chamberlain's mentioning me in a *Life* magazine article as part of a pro-Chinese Communist movement and implying that the State Department needed a housecleaning. And so it went, but in crescendo, for the next seven years.

Loyalty Boards were established in the government in 1947 to determine whether reasonable grounds existed for belief that the person involved was disloyal to the government of the United States. The investigative and security offices of the government collected derogatory information about employees, and when that material was deemed significant, the case was sent to the Loyalty Board for review. This first happened to me in 1949. The board met and I was cleared. I was not informed of these actions. As far as I know, there was no official scorecard kept on the number of probes I underwent. I counted eight on the basis of information released in the 1970s, but I am not sure that I detected them all. Of three I am certain, because they were hearings at which I was present.

Because of my belief that the government should be alert to subversive penetration of its ranks, I did not object to the grillings, even though they were not the way I would want to spend a holiday. I did think that the caliber of many engaged in this protection of our freedoms was well below par.

The principal charges against me, I learned later, came mainly from Hurley (probably planted on him by Soong) and from American Navy Captain, Milton Miles (inspired by Tai Li's secret police with whom he worked), and various American devotees of Chiang and his wife. These accusations were repeatedly dismissed until the rules were expanded beyond the test of loyalty. Under the expanded rules, an employee was culpable if he or she was branded as a security risk. One was a security risk if, for example, one was judged likely to disclose official secrets through indiscretion or intoxication, or if one had questionable contacts, political or sexual.

A select board, headed by the inspector general of the Army, General Daniel Noce, and four bureaucrats without experience in foreign affairs, finally found me not disloyal, but deficient in judgment, discretion, and reliability. So, in November 1954, John Foster Dulles fired me.

Before I was discharged, I wrote to General Noce on November 2, reviewing some points in my hearing that I thought needed elucidation. The first broad accusation made against me in the department's letter of charges was that "I actively opposed and sought to circumvent United States' policy toward China."

I continue now with excerpts from the letter to Noce:

> In an effort to clarify this issue, I would say that, up to the time of my departure from China, I understood the national policy of the United States in respect to China to be the traditional policy developed over one hundred years—embracing such doctrines as the equality of commercial opportunity, the "open door," and the preservation of China's territorial and administrative integrity—plus the wartime additions: that we should induce China to make a maximum contribution to the war strong, independent, and on our side. I was, of course, heartily in accord with this national policy.
>
> Implicit in our recognition of the National Government of China was a subsidiary policy of support of that government and its leader, Chiang Kai-shek. I do not remember any explicit statement issued by the United States Government to the effect that its policy was to support the National Government of China and Chiang Kai-shek. At the same time, I do not believe that the Board will find in any of my papers of the period under consideration any recommendation that the United States Government should withdraw support from the National Government of China or Chiang Kai-shek. I did believe, however, that the power relationship among the various Chinese factions was radically changing, that the National Government was steadily declining, that the Communists were steadily gaining, and that this trend was not likely to be reversed

by anything we would be willing to do. Holding inflexibly to a policy that seemed doomed to collapse, I thought, would lead to serious damage to American national interests.

I then explicitly described the ethical and practical dilemma that faces any diplomat who tries to do his job in such a situation:

> When a Foreign Service officer concludes that a policy is likely to betray our national interests, he can reason to himself that, as ultimate responsibility for policy rests with the top officials of the Department, he need feel no responsibility for the course upon which we are embarked; furthermore, his opinions might be in error or misunderstood or misrepresented—and so the safest thing for a bureaucrat to do in such a situation is to remain silent. Or, a Foreign Service officer can speak out about his misgivings and suggest alternative policies, knowing that he runs serious personal risks in so doing. I spoke out.

Then, returning to the specific Chinese matter, I wrote:

> Subsidiary to the policy of inducing China to make a maximum contribution to the war against Japan was, as I recall and has been indicated, the policy of activating and supporting the maximum Chinese force, including Communist. . . . During my final months in China, the question was not whether the Communists should be armed but in what context. General Hurley's initial effort in this direction was in September and October 1944 in the framework of a united command. When that failed, he sought to create a coalition so that the Communists would be enabled to fight the Japanese more effectively—with our aid. The arming of the Communists was, I gather, also involved in a proposal advanced by General Wedemeyer's Chief of Staff, as a result of which General Hurley denounced that honorable officer to the President as disloyal. The Board is familiar with my suggestion that the Communists be armed and is aware that it was so heavily qualified as to be, in retrospect, non-operative. . . .
>
> By December, 1944, as I remember, General Hurley began to assert, without confirmation from Washington, that American policy was one of the unqualified support of the National Government of China and the Generalissimo. This was a policy which, as I have said, seemed to me to be full of danger to American interests. In

a sense, General Hurley was simply articulating a hitherto accepted assumption. On the other hand, it could be said that he was enunciating a policy just at the time when its validity, its basis in the realities of a rapidly shifting situation, had become questionable.

General Wedemeyer assumably issued various directives to those under his command during the period I served him. I recall none.

I knew that General Wedemeyer wished to improve relations between the American headquarters and the Chinese military and civilian authorities. I was warmly in accord with this new approach, but I did not think that an essentially superficial change of this character would check the organic decay of the Nationalist position. While I was in full agreement with General Wedemeyer's wishes, I did not understand that they were meant to stop me from continuing to speak frankly in my contacts with American press representatives. I did not believe in misleading the American press—and through it the American public—nor do I think General Wedemeyer would have wished me to do so. . . .

All of this, of course, raised a larger question:

May I turn to the question of whether I was the leading proponent in the Department (presumably 1947–51) of the separability of the Chinese Communists from Moscow? This is a serious question. It touches upon one of the most important, if not the crucial problem confronting American diplomacy. If in our struggle with the Soviet world we are to win out without resort to war, a split in the Soviet-Chinese bloc would seem to be an essential prerequisite. Short of the overthrow of the Soviet regime, the most devastating political defeat that the USSR could suffer would be Peking's defection from Moscow's camp. And if war were to occur, it can scarcely be denied that to have China standing aside from the conflict would be of considerable help to us.

Ten years ago, I believed that it was essential to our national interests to prevent the creation of a Soviet-Chinese bloc. After the bloc was formed, I believed—and continue to believe—that one of the major objectives of American grand strategy should be the fission of the Soviet-Chinese structure.

But the domestic political agitation over the "loss" of China, the understandable public shock over the discovery that there had been Soviet penetration of the American Government, and the defeatist assumption that the Communist camp is indivisible meant that the question of separating Peking from Moscow was explored only skittishly and no effort was made to bring about a separation. Perhaps it is fortunate that such was the case. Or, perhaps, we lost an opportunity to bring about a massive defection in the Soviet Empire which would have shaken the Kremlin to its foundations and immeasurably improved our power position.

The answer to the original question is that I was not the leading proponent in the Department of State of the separability of the Chinese Communists from Moscow. I knew no proponents of such a dogma. I did believe, however, that certain factors suggested such a possibility and that the question should be examined. I am not surprised that I have been denounced for this.

Another serious charge occurred over the difficult problem facing any diplomat who must make reports and hazard estimates even though all the facts are never completely available. I responded by saying:

On the question of my reporting about China, I was asked whether some of my estimates were based on insufficient evidence. I agreed that they were.

In so answering, I was applying perfectionist standards to myself. I was harsher toward myself than I think I would be toward others.

It is true that, ideally, a Foreign Service officer should wait until all of the evidence is in before making a judgement, but it is often the case, as in a battle, that to wait for all of the intelligence to come in is to be paralyzed while decisive events pass one by.

I felt that the Board was troubled by the estimate I made of the Chinese Communists, politically and militarily. While the evidence was inadequate, it was all that I had. The urgency and gravity of the crisis which I believed to be descending upon us caused me to come to conclusions more quickly than I would have, had I not felt that time was so short. For the same reason, I stated my position more flatly than I otherwise would have.

Had I been more deliberate, had I waited for all the evidence to come in, I would not have made some of the errors evident in my memoranda. Nor would I have predicted well ahead of the events that, for example, the USSR would move into Central Europe, that it would enter the Pacific war for its own strategic purposes, that a Soviet-Chinese bloc would ensue, that our strategic position in the Pacific would be critically affected when we again found ourselves at war in the Far East—when none of these ideas were finding general acceptance at that time among most other Americans. Instead, I would have, along with my compatriots, watched events overtake evidence.

In short, there do occur situations in which, if one is to anticipate events (which is expected of Foreign Service officers) and not function as a historian, one must speak up on the basis of inadequate evidence.

The Board also seemed to me to be concerned over my submission of unevaluated reports, what is now termed raw intelligence, without labeling them as such or otherwise warning the Department that I was not underwriting all that was reported. This concern, I neglected to observe in my testimony, seemed to me to be based on unfamiliarity with the traditional form of reporting in the Foreign Service. This reporting was a development of the classical diplomatic correspondence, which was often personal and discursive. The traditional exchanges between officials abroad and officials in the Department of State were between men who were often personally as well as officially acquainted with one another and who, therefore, were able to communicate back and forth with great intelligibility, yet without categorizing and labelling every paragraph. And each tended to make mental adjustments in his evaluations of what the other wrote, on the basis of his familiarity with the correspondent.

In modern diplomacy, the press often plays a highly significant role. Hence arose the concern over my relationships with journalists. I responded:

> My contacts with the press during the war years in Chungking were largely confined to the American representatives of the American press. I saw them regularly. The theory given circulation in recent years that they were a clique is, in my opinion not valid, excepting as their living in the Chinese Government's Press Hostel forced them to reside together. Most were, so far as I could tell, able, well-informed, individualistic, patriotic Americans. That they came to the conclusion that things were going badly in China was no more than a recognition of facts that confronted one at every turn.
>
> These press representatives were well aware of not only the situation which confronted American officials in China but also the issues of American policy. This situation was not unique in Chung-

king—I subsequently found it to be the case elsewhere in the world. In my relations with the American newsmen in Chungking I therefore did not insult their intelligence nor provoke their contempt for official American understanding by pretending that the situation was other than it was. My comments to them were, I believe, sober, discreet, and moderate. And, as the Board knows, this briefing was not on my own initiative, but on standing instructions. Thinking back over this relationship, I remember no leaks of official secrets from me. When one looks over the Washington scene, this is not an inconsiderable record.

Wherever they are stationed, diplomats must also face the difficulty of choosing whether or not to talk with those who may be out of power at the time or may be opponents of the existing regime. Does one establish contact with either existing or potential adversaries or not? I answered as follows:

Next—my relations with the Chinese Communists. I cultivated them. I did so for a purpose—to obtain information. I did so with the knowledge of my superiors and my American colleagues. It was an open relationship.

I hope that the trouble I have gotten into on this account will not deter other Foreign Service officers from developing and working Communist contacts. If they fail to do so, we shall have by our own action closed our eyes to close inspection of the enemy. The risks are real—not only that the Communist contacts play their practiced role of provocateurs—attempting to compromise the officer in the eyes of his own colleagues and superiors—also that he is misinterpreted and denounced by ignorant or unscrupulous fellow-countrymen. But these are risks that must, in the national interest, be taken—with the support of the top official of the Department.

[Another] issue regarding contacts is that raised by the list of names which, in my letter of charges, I was asked to speak to. It is an issue which has become vital—although not fully recognized—in our national life. Simply stated, it is the issue between the judgement of the individual citizen and that of the Government on whether certain of his contacts may be, in varying degrees, pro-Communist.

Now a number of people on the list presented to me are known Communists. Other were open fellow-travellers.

But some are persons who, aside from being listed as suspect or worse, I have no reason to believe are disloyal. Everything I personally know of these individuals indicates that they are decent, patriotic Americans.

Furthermore there are reasons based on my own experience over many years that cause me to hesitate to accept the derogatory assumptions at face value. I know that it takes misrepresentation or defamation by but one person to start governmental suspicion and mistrust. I know that denunciation inspires denunciation. I know that a grotesquely sinister picture of a man can be developed by this process. I know that the individual accused, especially if he is a private citizen, does not realize, until he is formally charged, the full scope of the accusations against him. I know that the accused is not told who all of his accusers are. (I am aware of who one of mine was only because, by accident, I saw him slinking in to testify "confidentially" about me.) I know that not all investigators are qualified for their jobs. And I know that easily disprovable derogatory material is without apparent check introduced into a man's file, and that he can be charged on that basis, and that it is up to him to disprove the calumny.

So I may, perhaps be forgiven if, when I am questioned about some of my contacts, I hesitate to agree that because there is derogatory information about them in the security files they are automatically to be regarded as pariahs. And when I am pressed to declare more positively under oath my uncertain misgivings about a man, it is perhaps understandable that I have come to be squeamish about leveling the finger of accusation at, and thereby gravely injuring, one who may be blameless.

But this is only one side of the dilemma—the side of traditional American belief in friendship, fair play, and Christian respect for the individual.

On the other side, is the necessity that a free society protect itself against the Communist conspiracy. This necessity I recognize and strongly believe in—the more so because of my firsthand experience in observing and reporting on it from our Embassy in Moscow. The subtlety of this conspiracy and the subversion that it induces in our own society require, in my opinion, extraordinary measures to combat them. It is because I consider the Communist menace to be more subtly sinister than is generally recognized that I welcome the searching examination of my case made by the Board.

As I have testified, I believe that, as a Government servant, I must subordinate my judgement about my contacts to that of the Government. I may not agree with the security agents of the Government that certain of my contacts are not suitable, but if the decision is that they are—then, so long as I am an employee of the Government, I accept that decision.

One of the difficulties for a Foreign Service officer in the present system is, as I inadequately explained in my testimony, that he is not officially informed what contacts are unsuitable. A Foreign Service officer can be, until he is suddenly accused, unaware that certain of his contacts are regarded by the Government as unsuitable, and he does not know with what degree of disfavor, if any, certain people who have been publicly attacked are viewed by the security officials. For if a Foreign Service officer must sever connections with everyone, American and foreign, about whom there has been or may be a derogatory report, then he will, of necessity, live in a useless vacuum. This additional occupational hazard to a foreign service officer and his family needs to be seriously studied and a solution sought. . . .

I concluded then, and conclude now, with the following words:

Surely, one of our greatest needs now in this time of peril is that Americans stand together. And while we must be vigilant and stern in defense of our security against the wiles and violence of the enemy, it seems to me that we must also remember and nourish the diversity and spontaneity which have made us inventive, productive, and strong. For it is in this flux of freedom that our creativeness—and thus our positive security—has resided.

So we have a precarious balance to maintain—between restraint and liberty. The maintenance of this balance is a problem we have always had, but never in such crucial terms. For to lower our guard is to expose ourselves to infiltration and subversion, while to make restraints on liberty the main objective of security is to risk sterilization of our creativity and to pattern ourselves on the enemy— thus ceding him the easiest victory of all.

RAYMOND F. WYLIE
AND
IMMANUEL C.Y. HSU

3
The China Hands in Historical and Comparative Perspective

The American China Hands

The American China Hands of the 1940s deserve our continuing attention for a number of reasons. Their experience can tell us much about Chinese politics, American foreign policy, and the limitations faced by diplomats caught between the policies of governments and their own understanding of specific historical situations. The Foreign Service officers stationed in China found themselves caught between the policies of their own government and those of their Chinese hosts and what they considered to be the proper way to proceed. Their own government, for example, saw China as but one part of its larger geopolitical concerns and global foreign policy; events within China were subordinated to this larger picture and significant only to the extent that they influenced it. The Chinese government clearly possessed another set of interests. For it, internal developments were of paramount importance and foreign policy issues were usually interpreted in light of their potential impact on the political situation at home. For their own part, the China Hands believed that they had an ethical obligation to report events as they saw them. Their views, however, were largely determined by their own predilections and their own local—rather than global—views from the Chinese outpost itself.

The China Hands' agitation for a radical new foreign policy based on their pragmatic observation of the Chinese situation irritated the host government while finding only limited acceptance at home. Chiang Kai-shek, like his predecessors, therefore asked President Franklin D. Roosevelt to send personal emissaries to China, for he wanted a direct pipeline to the White House in order to bypass the resident diplomats. The empirical reporting of the China Hands necessarily reflected a local perspective, in which China loomed large in U.S. foreign policy calculations. But Washington assessed the Chinese situation in a global context and decided that what happened in China was not worth the risk of substantial military involvement. The clash of their own local views with the global perspective of the State Department thus placed the Foreign Service officers in a most difficult position.

To understand this problem more fully, we need to recognize that the geopolitical position of the United States made it necessary for Washington to seek a partner in East Asia and the Western Pacific who could serve as an anchor for American strategic and economic interests in that region. As early as 1939, for example, Treasury Department officials openly stated that postwar China "will make a wonderful future market for American goods and enterprise."[1] From the time of Pearl Harbor in December 1941 the United States generally assumed that because of its long struggle against Japan, China would emerge at the center of any postwar arrangement. In particular, President Roosevelt desired "a united, democratically progressive, and cooperative China"[2] capable of serving as a counterweight to the Soviet Union and open to the penetration of U.S. commerce and capital.

However, China's strategic importance to the Allies fell precipitously after the Cairo Conference in November 1943. Until that time, the Americans had seriously considered using eastern China as a staging ground from which to invade Japan. But this strategy was dropped at the Cairo Conference in favor of approaching Japan directly from the Pacific. The military function of the China theater of war thus was reduced to distracting and drawing off Japanese troops from U.S. operations in the Pacific. In 1944 George C. Marshall, head of the Joint Chiefs of Staff, instructed General Joseph Stilwell in China that "Japan should be defeated without undertaking a major campaign against her on the mainland of Asia, if her defeat could be accomplished in this manner."[3] To speed up the victory and save American lives, the United States decided to draw the Russians into the war against Japan and also to establish useful contacts with the Chinese Communists.

In the spring of 1945, Secretary of the Navy James Forrestal asked Secretary of War Henry Stimson: "What is our policy on Russian influence in the Far East? Do we desire a counterweight to that influence? And should it be China or should it be Japan?"[4] Although there was little doubt in Washington that a counterweight to Soviet power was indeed necessary, opinions were divided as to which nation should play the role. Before leaving office in 1944, for example, Secretary of State Cordell Hull thought that China had only a fifty-fifty chance of becoming a great power.[5] And his successor, Joseph Grew, proposed a revitalized Japan as a desirable option should China prove unable to fulfill its assigned role.[6] Even though no definite decision was reached at that time, it was obvious that if China could fit into American plans in the postwar period, Nanking deserved support; if not, a revitalized Japan could equally serve as the cornerstone for U.S. interests in East Asia.

But the United States was determined not to become deeply involved in a Chinese civil war in the pursuit of its foreign policy goals in Asia. Washington adopted a policy of mediating between the Nationalists and the Communists and urging Chiang Kai-shek to renovate his government in order to outflank the Communists via reform. However, Chiang did not carry out the promised reforms and refused to reach a political settlement with the Communists. This prompted U.S. Foreign Service officers to air their belief that China's future was not Chiang's but Mao Tse-tung's, and as discussed throughout this volume, they urged Washington to adopt a policy of realism toward the possibility of a Communist victory in the spreading civil war in China.

After the failure of the Marshall Mission in January 1947, Washington had all but given up hope for Chiang and the Nationalists. In May 1947, for example, the Joint Chiefs placed China very low (fourteenth) on the list of countries that should receive American assistance.[7] As Chiang relentlessly pursued a military solution to China's political problems, he ripped apart the fragile fabric of postwar Chinese society and undermined his chance of serving as the anchor for U.S. interests in East Asia. Meanwhile, in the second half of 1947, Washington decided to slow down the pace of social reforms in Japan and to rebuild that country as an alternative base for American power in East Asia. Such an effort, it was argued, would entail far less commitment of resources than would be the case for China and would offer more assurance of success. Thus Japan emerged as America's main partner in East Asia and the Pacific, and in 1952 a U.S.-Japan Security Treaty formalized the new relationship. In the meantime, China, after the Communist victory in 1949, had allied itself to the Soviet Union under the terms of the Sino-Soviet Treaty of 1950.

Chiang erroneously assumed that the United States would not tolerate the Communists as his successors, though there was nothing in U.S. policy that should realistically have led him to think that Washington would support his regime if it proved unable to fulfill its assigned role. From the American standpoint, the rise of the Communist People's Republic of China (PRC) was not acceptable, nor was its alliance with the Soviet Union. Yet, in light of the inability of the United States to influence the course of events in China, the unacceptable had to be tolerated. Still, Washington took consolation in the belief that the new regime's pressing domestic problems ensured that China would not constitute a serious military threat for many years to come.

As potential allies in the postwar era, China and the United States proved to be grave disappointments to each other. Washington grew increasingly exasperated at the inability of the Nationalists to translate their economic and military superiority over the Chinese Communist Party (CCP) into victory in the civil war of 1946–1949. Nanking in turn resented what it perceived as lukewarm American political support and niggardly military assistance. The Communists, of course, loudly protested any amount of aid at all to the Nationalist Party— the Kuomintang (KMT). By late 1949, the earlier expectations of postwar cooperation between the two countries had been replaced with bitterness and recriminations on all sides. As catalysts for change in U.S. policy during these tumultuous years, the China Hands had perhaps succeeded more in exposing the shortcomings of the KMT, America's ally, than in convincing Washington and the American public of the Communists' virtues. Thus, they were susceptible to the charge that their "pro-Communist, anti-KMT" attitudes and reporting helped bring about the stunning reversal of U.S. policy in China during the critical civil war period.

The particular difficulty faced by the American China Hands of the 1940s, although certainly unique in some regards, possesses a number of historical precedents. As catalysts for change in China, the Foreign Service officers invariably found themselves in a difficult position vis-à-vis the Chinese government and their own government as well. This was not the first time that such a phenomenon had occurred.

The British "Old China Hands"

Take, for instance, the British "Old China Hands" of the mid and late nineteenth century. They were mostly traders, consular officers, soldiers of fortune, journalists, and missionaries. Most of them had gained access to China as a result of the Opium War of 1839–1842, which led to the signing of the Treaty of Nanking in the latter year. The treaty in effect "opened" China to growing British and other foreign influence and provided for the establishment of five treaty ports in which foreigners could legally trade. But these Old China Hands grew progressively discontent with the status quo, believing that their treaty rights were insufficient and not always enforced by the Chinese government (the Ch'ing, or Manchu, dynasty).

By the mid-1850s foreign sentiment in the treaty ports was overwhelmingly in favor of change. Then, in 1856, a sudden outbreak of hostilities between Great Britain and China (over a jurisdictional dispute involving the *Arrow,* a Chinese sailing vessel with British registry) provided an opportunity for the foreigners to press the case for treaty revision. They vigorously pushed for the greater opening of China, for more treaty ports, more railways, more mining and telegraphic concessions, more inland navigation, and more freedom for religious propagation. They justified their demands in the name of progress and considered the "opening of China" well worth the risk of destabilizing the Chinese government. For their part, the Chinese rulers were determined to resist any further foreign encroachments on their sovereignty and appointed a determined new official, Yeh Ming-ch'en, to keep the Western powers in check.

The Western powers, however sympathetic they were to the case for treaty revision, did not wish to bring about the downfall of the

Ch'ing dynasty that had ruled China since 1644. The British, in particular, had no intention actually to colonize China and turn it into a second India. Great Britain viewed relations with China as but one part of its foreign policy and had to consider the impact of Chinese developments upon its larger global concerns. For this reason, the British sent Lord Elgin to China in 1857 after the outbreak of the so-called Arrow War (or second Anglo-Chinese War) to assess their larger interests. He was appalled at the behavior of the fiery consuls, the aggressive traders, and the haughty missionaries whom he saw in the treaty ports. After witnessing the injustices being visited upon the hapless Chinese by British consuls and traders, he wrote to his wife: "I thought bitterly of those who, for the most selfish objects are trampling under foot this ancient civilization. . . . Certainly I have seen more to disgust me with my fellow countrymen than I saw during the whole course of my previous life."[8] In particular, he called the British consul at Canton, Harry Parkes, "very bloody," "violent and domineering," and "the very incarnation of the man on the spot" dominated by the immediate facts before his eyes.[9]

Nonetheless, London had by this time determined on treaty revision, and Elgin was instructed to take whatever steps he deemed necessary to achieve this end. Between 1857 and 1860, in cooperation with the French, the British inflicted a series of military defeats on China and forced the signing of the Treaty of Tientsin in 1858, which was subsequently ratified in 1860. Elgin remained uneasy throughout the protracted negotiations, fearing that if he succeeded in further opening China to Western influence, the new privileges thus won would be abused by people like Parkes and the other Old China Hands. For this reason he insisted on the right of official diplomatic residence in Peking—not only to force the Ch'ing government to take up foreign affairs directly but also to use the resident minister to restrain the behavior of the consuls, traders, and missionaries in Canton and other treaty ports.

At a party given in Elgin's honor by the leading British firms in China at the time (Jardine Matheson and Dent and Beale, among others), the hosts expressed a hope that "the result of Your Excellency's exertions, we trust, may be more fully to develop the vast resources of China, and to extend among the people the elevating influences of a higher civilization." Elgin reminded them that Chinese civilization was ancient and not one of "barbarism," and though in many respects "effete and imperfect," it was not "without claims on our sympathy and respect."[10] He admonished the Old China Hands to make judicious use of their newly won rights: "Neither our own conscience nor the judgment of mankind will acquit us if, when we are asked to what use we have turned our opportunities, we can only say that we have filled our pockets from among the ruins which we have found or made."[11]

In the case of Lord Elgin, we see that the chief spokesman of the British government in China had a very low opinion of many of the British residents in the treaty ports. He found them too aggressive, too pushy, too anxious to state their own positions, and too inclined to be independent of their own government. Colonial Secretary Lord Stanley viewed them in the same light. He warned them on several occasions that if they pursued their own policies and desires for concessions too aggressively, it might well result in the dismemberment of China. And he cautioned them: "We must not expect the Chinese, either the Government or the people, at once to see things in the same light as we see them; we must bear in mind that we have obtained our knowledge by experience extending over many years, and we must lead and not force the Chinese to the adoption of a better system."[12]

The Old China Hands did not appreciate such lecturing, and they reacted with suspicion, hostility, and arrogance. They had no kind words for Lord Elgin, the foreign secretary, the colonial secretary, or many others in the government back in London. They ridiculed their own leaders as ignorant of the Chinese situation and clamored for a civil service examination for British envoys and for foreign and colonial secretaries, to make sure they had "full knowledge of the people and countries they are called on to have dealings with."[13]

This mutual antipathy between the British Old China Hands and their government representatives responsible for China policy reflects the perennial problem of reconciling local and global perspectives and interests. The resident China Hands obviously were more knowledgeable about China than London-based or visiting officials; equally, however, they often judged specific situations on the basis of a local perspective and failed to grasp the wider dimensions of British foreign policy, in which China occupied a secondary position. Under these circumstances their policy recommendations, although based on firsthand observation and experience, were more often than not out of touch with broader, more generalized views of political and government leaders back in England. In general, their views were more intense, and their recommendations more aggressive, than those of their fellow countrymen who were far removed from the China scene. Their personal lives and economic well-being were closely linked to the further "opening" of the moribund Chinese empire, and they did not shrink from advocating a tough-minded, aggressive policy to this effect. Certain members of the Old China Hands did indeed counsel moderation in Anglo-Chinese relations, but they were usually a distinct minority or in any event not as vocal as their more strident colleagues.

An American "Old China Hand"

There is no better illustration of the potential for friction between the resident China Hands, their home governments, and the Chinese authorities than the case of Dr. Peter Parker. Arriving in Canton in 1834, fresh from Yale Medical School, Parker quickly established himself as the founder of medical missions in China. But he eventually abandoned his medical concerns for a career as a missionary-diplomat, serving successively from 1844 on as interpreter, secretary, chargé d'affaires, and ultimately commissioner at the U.S. legation in Canton.[14] Peter Parker was a strong advocate of the view that the outbreak of the Taiping Rebellion in 1850 gave the Western powers an excellent opportunity to press for an extension of their treaty privileges vis-à-vis the embattled Ch'ing dynasty. Thus, upon his appointment as United States commissioner in China in September 1855, he embarked on an ambitious course of action that was to dominate Sino-American relations for the term of his office.

Parker had a wealth of experience of both China and the foreign diplomatic service in China, for his combined service as legation secretary, chargé d'affaires, and commissioner was longer than all the terms of the previous commissioners put together. He could also speak and read Chinese fluently and was well grounded in Chinese history and customs. In spite of these obvious qualifications for the post, however, his missionary zeal, aggressive attitude toward China, and ignorance of American and European diplomacy combined to render him ill equipped to formulate a China policy appropriate to the interests of his country.[15] Parker's virtual "adventurism" in dealing with China forced Washington, which had been rather passive in its concern with China up to that time, to take policy formulation out of the hands of the resident envoys in China. Indeed, Parker's term as commissioner marked the turning point in the formulation of U.S. policy toward China.

Secretary of State William L. Marcy gave Parker essentially the same instructions as those of his predecessor, Robert M. McLane: (1) to work for treaty revision, and (2) to cooperate with the other Western powers, short of armed aggression. With the blessing of the Department of State, Parker stopped off at London and Paris on his way to China to consult with Lord Clarendon, the British foreign secretary, and Count Walewski, his French counterpart, on the possibilities of joint action. Parker was favorably received at both capitals and continued on to China confident that a joint project was feasible. Indeed, during the interview in London, Clarendon had expressed the firm conviction that "not only do our consciences approve, but the whole world must commend our policy."[16] After arriving in China in late 1855, however, Parker found the British and French envoys surprisingly cool to his proposals for joint action against China. But Parker's plans received new encouragement with the outbreak of the Arrow War in October 1856. This led to the British occupation of Canton and a sudden revival in British consul Sir John Bowring's interest in the possibilities of American and French cooperation against the Chinese. Accordingly, Parker wrote Marcy on December 12, 1856, proposing a definite course of action: First, a joint expedition by Britain, the United States, and France should be undertaken to north China in order to force the Chinese to concede to treaty revision; then, if the expedition was unsuccessful, the British should occupy the Chusan Islands, the French Korea, and the Americans Formosa (Taiwan) until such time as favorable terms were had from Peking. In language that is particularly quaint, Parker proposed a "concurrent policy with England and France in China, not an alliance, but independent and distinct action, yet similar, harmonious, and simultaneous."[17]

Parker's proposal that the United States should occupy the island of Formosa, an integral part of China, was much more than a mere tactical move to bring about treaty revision. In 1854 Commodore Matthew C. Perry had sent a fact-finding expedition to Formosa and at the time had spoken of the necessity of extending the "territorial jurisdiction" of the United States to Formosa. Parker, who shared Perry's interest in the fate of the island, was greatly influenced by the opinions of Gideon Nye, Jr., and W. M. Robinet, two American merchant-adventurers who were active in Formosa. On February 10, 1867, Nye wrote to Parker suggesting the desirability of some kind of American protectorate over all or part of the island. Parker agreed and forwarded Nye's letter to the Department of State, expressing the hope that "the government of the United States may not *shrink* from the action." On March 2 of the same year Robinet also wrote Parker, suggesting that if outright annexation should prove impossible, "it would advance the cause of humanity, religion, and civilization" if the U.S. government would give protection to Americans who should erect an independent government on Formosa. Much enthused by the whole idea, Parker wrote the secretary of state on March 10, 1857, pointing out that in his opinion Formosa "may not long remain a portion of the empire of China . . . and in the event of its being severed from the empire politically, as it is geographically, that the United States should possess it is obvious, particularly as respects the great principle of balance of power."[18]

By the spring of 1857, therefore, events in China were on the point of getting out of hand, and Washington was called upon to take some decisive steps concerning relations with China. As William B. Reed, Parker's successor as U.S. envoy, was later to inform the secretary of state, the archives of the legation showed that Parker, "to a certain point, encouraged Sir John Bowring (and others) in the most extravagant expectations of cooperation on our part, to the extent even of acquisition of territory."[19] Although Parker's specific proposals for the annexation of Formosa did not reach Washington until the summer of 1857, the authorities there had been aware for some time of Perry's and Parker's interest in the island. The issue was given immediate urgency by press reports that alleged that both the U.S. consular service and the naval squadron in the area had directly participated in the British assault on Canton. An immediate investigation was ordered that clearly established, at the very least, that the sympathies of the resident Americans were plainly with their British kinsmen.[20]

On top of all this, the authorities in Washington (like their successors during the 1940s) were being pressed by various domestic interest groups to take a firm stand in China. The British and French representatives in the capital were urging U.S. participation in a joint effort, and the China merchants in the United States (whose attitude toward China had been hardening) came out in favor of such cooperation. On April 2, 1857, Gerard Hallock, the editor of a commercial newspaper, wrote Marcy that "if any one of the three nations were to undertake the negotiation alone, John Chinaman might be tempted to resist."[21] As far as most missionaries were concerned, their general attitude was well reflected in the opinions of Peter Parker himself. In spite of these multiple pressures urging war, however, President Franklin Pierce and Secretary of State Marcy refused to be drawn along. In the first place, they did not believe that U.S. relations with China, even though far from satisfactory, warranted actual armed conflict. In the second place, they fully realized that the threat of civil war in American itself precluded any possibility that Congress would approve involvement in a war in distant China.

Accordingly, Marcy wrote Parker on February 27, 1857, rejecting the latter's advocation of aggressive action as a "last resort." "The 'last resort' means war," said Marcy, "and the Executive branch of this government is not the war-making power."[22] Having decided against close cooperation with Britain and France in a move against China, Pierce and Marcy took pains to ensure that their successors would pursue the same policy. Their efforts were successful, for on April 5, 1857, after leaving office, Pierce wrote Marcy: "I was glad to receive your note of the 3rd inst., and to learn that our policy in regard to affairs in China is not to be departed from."[23] This concern on the part of Pierce and Marcy is significant, for it is the only instance to date of an outgoing president's concern over the continuation of his China policy by his successor.

Unlike most of his predecessors, President James Buchanan had served a term as secretary of state and was relatively informed as to the situation in China. As a result, Buchanan took the control of foreign policy into his own hands and was not inclined to seek out the opinions of the merchants and missionaries as to the correct policy toward China, as earlier presidents had done. Being in general agreement with the policy of Pierce and Marcy, Buchanan on April 10, 1857, formally rejected the British and French overtures seeking American support in a joint venture in China. And a week or so later, on April 22, William B. Reed was appointed to replace Parker as U.S. representative in China. Reed was the first person since Caleb Cushing, the American diplomat who negotiated the Sino-U.S. Treaty of Wanghsia in 1844, to be invested with the powers of envoy extraordinary and minister plenipotentiary. He was thus in a position to sign a new, revised treaty should the opportunity arise.

Indeed, on the desirability of negotiating a new treaty with China, President Buchanan was in complete agreement with Peter Parker. Unlike Parker, however, Buchanan did not feel that the situation warranted aggressive action against Peking. In the "most detailed instructions since Cushing," Buchanan and Secretary of State Lewis Cass acknowledged to the new envoy that "your position is a delicate one and will require the exercise of your best discretion."[24] Still, they made it clear to Reed that his efforts in China "must be confined to firm representations, appealing to the justice and policy of the Chinese authorities, and leaving to your own Government to determine upon the course to be adopted, should your representatives be fruitless."[25]

Parker's "aggressive policy" was thus decisively repudiated, and upon the arrival of his official notice of recall in early August 1857, he and his wife left China for good and settled into retirement in Washington, D.C. Although he was respected as one of the nation's most knowledgeable and experienced "China Hands," he never again played an influential role in determining the course of U.S. policy toward China.

This discussion clearly demonstrates the difficult position of the British and American Old China Hands vis-à-vis their own government and diplomatic leaders, who often considered them overly aggressive toward China and ignorant of the broader foreign policy concerns of their home capitals. In many cases, as with Peter Parker, the home government came to exert a greater degree of control over the resident diplomats, thus allowing them less freedom of action in their Chinese outpost. As for the Chinese government, it eventually tired of the constant agitation for concessions from the Old China Hands and decided to bypass them completely by sending out diplomats to appeal directly to the foreign governments concerned.[26] With the establishment of official embassies abroad, China entered the modern international system and quickly established a role in global politics that far exceeded any conceptions of the Old China Hands during the nineteenth century.

It would seem, then, that the experience of the American China Hands of the 1940s was not entirely dissimilar from that of some of their British and American predecessors nearly a century earlier. Caught between the interests and policies of the Chinese government and their home authorities, they sought to devise an activist, assertive policy that proved to be at odds with both sides, and in the end they were bypassed or dismissed. What is unusual in the case of the 1940s, however, is the fate that befell these officials upon their return to the United States. At no time before or since the McCarthyist era have American diplomats been subjected to the kind of ideological and administrative persecution suffered by the China Hands after their return home. Yet, the historical record does suggest a close parallel, namely, the experience of the Soviet advisers in China in the mid-1920s and their subsequent repression following the collapse of Soviet policy in 1927. Closer examination of these two historical episodes suggests a similarity that has hitherto been neglected in the scholarly literature.

The Soviet "China Hands"

Lenin and the other Bolshevik leaders, after the consolidation of their power in the Soviet Union in 1920, began to take a great interest in developments in China. Prospects for the "permanent revolution" in Europe looked bleak by this time, and it was hoped that the rising tide of nationalism in the new Chinese republic would help ignite a massive antiimperialist movement throughout the colonial world. But the political sitution in China was highly complex and not easily susceptible to effective outside manipulation: Warlords who controlled Peking and much of the north were recognized by the foreign powers as the legitimate Chinese government for purposes of official diplomatic relations. Other warlords dominated most of central China, usually enjoying the support of one foreign power or another but owing no allegiance to Peking. In the south, Sun Yat-sen was desperately trying to weld the Nationalist Party into a force capable of mounting a "northern expedition" to destroy the warlords and unite China under a single government. Many disaffected intellectuals and students, on the other hand, sought their country's salvation in alliance with the newly established Soviet Union and the Communist International. In July 1921, with the assistance of Comintern representatives G. M. Voitinsky and H. Sneevliet, among others, a small group of these radical elements met to found the Chinese Communist Party.[27]

Yet, Moscow believed that its best chances of influencing political developments in China lay not with the fledgling CCP, but rather with Sun Yat-sen and the Nationalists. In January 1923, Sun and Soviet diplomat A. A. Joffe signed a joint agreement whereby the Soviets would provide Sun and the KMT with political and military assistance in their mission to unite China. A "united front" with the CCP was declared, with both Chinese parties agreeing to bury their political differences in the interests of a successful military campaign against the northern warlords. Fundamental to the agreement was Moscow's promise to dispatch to China official advisers (*sovetniki*) in a wide range of functions pertaining to the political and military reorganization of the KMT and its cooperation with the CCP. Thus, there arrived in Canton during the period 1923–1927 a sizable number of Soviet and Comintern advisers headed by M. M. Borodin. Borodin was an "Old Bolshevik" who had spent over ten years in exile in the United States, subsequently working with Communist movements in countries ranging from England to Mexico.[28] Despite certain political differences between them, Borodin quickly won the confidence of Sun and proceeded to place advisers in a number of key positions within the KMT party and army organizations. It was from within this group that the Soviet Union was to develop its first generation of "China Hand" experts, although, as we shall see, many of them were to suffer a fate similar to that of the American China Hands of the 1940s.

Almost immediately, Borodin and his fellow advisers were caught in the middle of competing political forces within China, a situation exacerbated by conflicting policies emanating from Moscow. Essentially, the dilemma was this: The advisers had to promote the "proletarian" CCP and the cause of Marxist revolution in China, yet at the same time support the "bourgeois" KMT and its policy of national unification. As long as Sun was alive the inherent contradictions in this policy were held in check, but soon after his death in 1925 his successor, Chiang Kai-shek, turned against the CCP. In

April 1927, following a successful "northern expedition" against the warlords, Chiang systematically destroyed the Communists by means of wholesale massacre. Throughout the summer, despite an abortive mission to China by M. N. Roy, a senior Comintern spokesman, Chiang's rise to power proceeded apace. He neutralized the "leftist" faction within his own party, won grudging support from most of the major warlords, and ordered the expulsion of all Soviet influence from China.[29] Borodin and most of his fellow advisers left China by late summer 1927, and Chiang turned his attention to consolidating his new regime in Nanking and liquidating what remained of the indigenous Communist movement.

Based on their personal inclinations and actual experiences in China, most of the Soviet advisers during this period were suspicious of the "bourgeois" character of the KMT. Although not unaware of the limitations of the young CCP, they favored a policy of greater support for the Communists and the mass movements of workers and peasants. From the broader perspective of Soviet foreign policy, however, Stalin and the other Soviet leaders (including Trotsky and the opposition) decreed continuing support of the KMT. They believed it was critical to maintain a position of influence within the one political movement that held out the possibility of uniting China under a single government. When Trotsky ended his support for the KMT in the spring of 1927, Stalin refused to go along lest his China policy since 1923 be discredited, to the political advantage of his opponents in the fierce power struggle that was then engulfing the Kremlin. During his last year in China, even Borodin grew despondent, realizing that Moscow's continuing support for Chiang Kai-shek and the KMT was futile. He complained that his former revolutionary role had been reduced to the "protection of Russian interests" as defined by the Stalinist faction increasingly in control of Soviet foreign policy.[30]

Upon returning to the Soviet Union in 1927, many of these Soviet "China Hands" became involved in the bitter struggle between Stalin and Trotsky, in which the question of the success or failure of current China policy became an important bone of contention. Indeed, the contributions of these former advisers did much to enliven Soviet polemical and scholarly debates on China in the late 1920s and early 1930s. With Stalin's final triumph over Trotsky in the early 1930s, however, this impassioned debate was terminated in favor of an official line that vindicated Stalin's "correct" China policy and blamed the failure of the 1924–1927 revolution on the "immaturity" of the CCP itself. As the Soviet sinologist G. V. Efimov noted in 1967, the political climate after 1931 or so did not favor a continuation of these ongoing discussions of the 1924–1927 period, and they were thereupon "adjourned for 30 years," i.e., until after Stalin's death.[31]

Many, if not most, of the Soviet advisers in China during this period returned to the Soviet Union under a political cloud from which they never escaped. Some of the more prominent figures, such as M. M. Borodin, were relegated to minor administrative or educational posts for the rest of their careers. Others, like M. N. Roy, were expelled from the Comintern and thereupon lapsed into political obscurity. As for the less visible individuals, their fates were mixed; some weathered the storms and later rose to prominence, whereas others were not so fortunate. Many of the military advisers, including V. K. Blyukher, perished in the Stalinist purges in the late 1930s, and a generation of young sinologists such as M. I. Kazanin languished for years in labor camps until their rehabilitation in the 1950s.[32] Thus, although the subsequent fates of the American China experts of the 1940s and the Soviet China advisers of the 1920s are in some respects comparable, they are far from being identical. As Steven I. Levine has written in his introduction to the memoirs of V. V. Vishnyakova-Akimova, who served in China as an assistant to Borodin, "only through an act of imagination can we who know the numbing effect of McCarthyism in America on China studies even begin to grasp the consequences of Stalinism for Soviet China studies."[33]

A Comparative Perspective

For many of the Soviet advisers in the 1920s, as for the American and British Old China Hands of the 1850s and the U.S. Foreign Service officers of the 1940s, the essential predicament was similar. They were caught between the conflicting demands of the broader perspectives of their own government, the immediate needs of the current Chinese regime, and their own, more localized understanding of the issues at stake. This was certainly true of the Soviet advisers, most of whom were quite young when they went to China and were imbued with the hope of sparking off a Marxist revolution in that oppressed land. To them, what happened in China was central to the international proletarian revolution, and they tried to convey this sense of mission to Moscow. Yet, as Dan Jacobs has pointed out, these operations in China "were not given a high order of priority by either the Comintern or the Politburo," both of which placed greater importance on events in Europe and the West generally.[34] Thus, when forced to choose between supporting the KMT or the CCP, Stalin chose to maintain ties with Chiang Kai-shek. This was entirely in keeping with the main thrust of Soviet foreign policy, namely, to prevent China from falling under the exclusive domination of the Western powers and, increasingly, Japan. Consequently, many of the Soviet advisers found themselves at odds with the policies of both their own government and that of the Nationalists. After the final rupture between Moscow and Nanking, their position became untenable, and they were forced to leave China feeling a sense of betrayal by both sides.

It is perhaps interesting to speculate why the Soviet China advisers of the 1920s and the American China Hands of the 1940s fell afoul of powerful domestic forces upon their return home. This is in sharp contrast to the experience of the British and American Old China Hands of the previous century. Although many of them incurred official displeasure and were eventually transferred or recalled, they usually went on to pursue normal lives. Harry Parkes, the belligerent British consul, later distinguished himself as a diplomat in Japan, and the American missionary-diplomat Peter Parker lived out a lengthy and respected retirement back in the States. Yet, the experience of their twentieth-century American and Soviet counterparts was very different and one is forced to ask why. What factor can account for the persecution of the American and Soviet China Hands upon their return from lengthy and often dangerous assignments in the field?

It should be noted that to a certain degree the American and Soviet experience was unique, for by and large it was not replicated in other Western nations. Take Great Britain, for example, which had hundreds of its nationals residing in the nonoccupied parts of China in the 1940s. Many of them were in China in private capacities—as missionaries, teachers, businessmen, or journalists. But there were others serving at the official level in the diplomatic service, the consular corps, and the military, among others. This group even included a number of individuals who were of known radical leanings and even sympathetic to the Chinese Communist cause.[35] Yet, following the CCP victory in 1949, none of these former China Hands were subjected to the kind of persecution experienced by their American and Soviet counterparts. This may be explained in part by the greater capacity of British political culture for ideological diversity and tolerance, but there is another, more immediate, reason as well. By 1949, when the Chinese Communists seized power, Britain was no longer a major world power and was quickly realizing that its pretenses of extensive global influence were things of the past. In Asia, its perceived interests in China were minimal, apart from the colony of Hong Kong. Thus, London was prepared to recognize the new regime in China in order to protect Hong Kong and facilitate Britain's gradual withdrawal from Asia east of Suez. The Communist takeover had little impact on domestic politics, and impassioned debates over "who lost China" had little resonance in British public life in the early 1950s.[36]

The situation with the Soviet Union in the 1930s and the United States in the 1950s, however, was quite the opposite. Both nations saw themselves as powerful actors on the global scene, with a unique international mission and ideological role to fulfill in the newly awakening colonial world. Also, being Pacific nations, they had strong geopolitical and security interests in what happened in China and were prepared to intervene in pursuit of these interests. For Moscow in the 1920s, it was believed that the struggle between the northern warlords and their foreign backers, on the one hand, and the KMT and CCP, on the other, would determine China's political destiny for years to come. It was therefore deemed appropriate, in the pursuit of Russia's national and global interests, to attempt to influence the outcome of that struggle in Moscow's favor. Likewise, Washington agreed that the fate of China lay in the resolution of the long-standing conflict between the Nationalists and the Communists and was determined by intervention to tilt the balance of forces toward U.S. geopolitical and security goals. Yet, although the stakes were high, both powers grew to appreciate the limits of their ability to influence the course of events in so huge a country. When the real and anticipated costs began to outstrip the potential gains, both powers cut their losses and abruptly pulled back from further involvement in China's internal affairs.

By the time they withdrew, however, the "China issue" had become the subject of bitter contention at the highest level of politics in both Moscow and Washington. For Trotsky and the opposition, it was imperative to pin the blame for the "debacle in China" on Stalin, with whom they were contending for supreme power within the Soviet Union itself. Likewise, Republicans in the United States discovered in the "loss of China" an effective issue with which to attack the incumbent Democratic administration of Harry S. Truman. What distinguished these debates in both countries was their sharp ideological tone. Many of those involved in making or executing China policy were accused of ulterior political motives or of having been misled by others with such motives. Before long, former China Hands from both countries found themselves increasingly caught up in these domestic debates, in which they were to figure largely as scapegoats for foreign policy failures in China. In the Stalinist interpretation, the Soviet advisers had failed to understand the "bourgeois character" of the KMT and had thus exposed Soviet policy to attack and failure. The McCarthyists, on the other hand, claimed that many Foreign Service officers, journalists, and others had been duped into believing that the Chinese Communists were mere "agrarian reformers." Accordingly, they argued that the China Hands had provided Washington with faulty, if not outright deceitful, advice on events in China. Because of the heightened ideological climate and contending political forces in both countries during the respective historical periods, the retribution suffered by the China Hands was unusually harsh and vindictive. With the passage of time and the mellowing of ideological convictions, many of those unjustly treated were later rehabilitated or at least judged in a more objective and favorable light.

In retrospect, the China Hands ("old" and "new" equally) can be seen as transitional figures in China's anguished move from traditional isolationism to modern global involvement. There were, of course, resident foreigners in previous times; witness the European Jesuits of the sixteenth and seventeenth centuries. Likewise, there are thousands of foreigners in China today, encompassing a wide range of nationalities and activities of every description. Yet, there is a difference between the China Hands of the century between the

Opium War and the Communist victory (1839–1949) and those foreigners who preceded or followed them. In other historical periods, China was ruled by powerful regimes that were able to regulate the numbers and functions of the foreign China Hands. During the century of decline, many foreigners resident in China freed themselves from Chinese control by means of the "unequal treaties," with their guarantees of extraterritoriality and other privileges. To a significant degree, they were a law unto themselves and were able to act independently in the pursuit of their various enterprises in China. Not surprisingly, they frequently incurred suspicion and resentment on the part of many Chinese, officials and commoners alike, who regarded them as unwelcome and aggressive intruders. Hence, we see numerous "antiforeign" movements in China during this century, of which the Boxer Uprising of 1899–1901 is a good example. In many cases, including the Boxers, these popular outbursts were often aided and abetted by the Chinese authorities themselves.

As China disintegrated internally, successive generations of Chinese came to realize that the hated foreigners who had precipitated their decline could be used to good advantage as well. Numerous foreign China Hands were utilized by the Chinese at all levels as advisers, entrepreneurs, teachers, and physicians and in a host of other functional capacities, including diplomacy. But these activities did not take place in a politically neutral environment, and this was especially true following the disintegration of centralized government after the Revolution of 1911. The Peking warlords would consult one group of foreign advisers, other warlords another, the Nationalists another, and the Communists yet another. In most cases, the advisers were closely attached to the political, economic, and security interests of the various foreign powers involved in China. Thus, many of the China Hands—despite their frequent protestations of neutrality and desire to help China—could not but be closely associated in Chinese eyes, for better or worse, with the interests of their own nations rather than with those of China itself. Witness the bitter comments of Mao Tse-tung upon the departure in 1949 of John Leighton Stuart, the last U.S. ambassador to Chiang Kai-shek's China: "Leighton Stuart is an American born in China; he . . . spent many years running missionary schools in China; . . . he used to pretend to love both the United States and China and was able to deceive quite a number of Chinese. . . . Leighton Stuart has departed. . . . Very good. Very good. [This is an] event worth celebrating."[37]

Like Peter Parker in the nineteenth century, Stuart had devoted his life to China, combining both missionary and diplomatic careers in service to his Christian religion, his American homeland, and his adopted country. Although Mao's judgment was harsh, and perhaps unfair, it was not unreasonable in the eyes of the new Chinese rulers. In any event, Stuart's circumstance was not very different from that of many other China Hands throughout China's so-called "Century of Humiliation." When Mao declared on October 1, 1949, that the "Chinese people have stood up!" he rang down the curtain on the foreign China Hands represented by John Leighton Stuart and the others we have discussed. They had done much to influence the course of China's relations with the major foreign powers and to shape the ways in which Chinese and foreigners perceived each other during a hundred years of national and cultural confrontation. Now, finally, their role was over, and most of them left China for good, leaving behind a legacy that has yet to be fully explored by later generations.

Seen in historical and comprative perspective, then, the experience of the American China Hands of the 1940s is of considerable interest and significance. It demonstrates the precarious position of diplomats and others who are caught between the conflicting demands of their own government's policy, the interests of their host governments, their desire to do what they believe to be ethically proper, and their personal and often imperfect understanding of specific historical and local situations in which they find themselves. There is little doubt that the future will provide us with further examples of this perennial dilemma in the conduct of international diplomacy in an increasingly complex world.

Notes

1. U.S. Congress, Senate, Committee on the Judiciary, Internal Security Subcommittee, *Morgenthau Diary (China)*, 89th Congress, First Session (Washington, D.C.: Government Printing Office, 1965), p. 7.

2. Charles Romanus and Riley Sunderland, *Time Runs Out in CBI* (Washington, D.C.: Office of the Chief of Military History, 1959), p. 337.

3. Charles Romanus and Riley Sunderland, *Stilwell's Command Problems* (Washington, D.C.: Office of the Chief of Military History, 1956), pp. 363–364.

4. Walter Millis (ed.), *The Forrestal Diaries* (New York: Viking Press, 1951), p. 52.

5. Cordell Hull, *The Memoirs of Cordell Hull* (New York: Macmillan, 1948), pp. 1586–1587.

6. U.S. Congress, *Morgenthau Diary,* p. 1394.

7. U.S. Department of State, *Foreign Relations of the United States, 1947,* Vol. VII, *The Far East: China* (Washington, D.C.: Government Printing Office, 1972), pp. 853–854.

8. Letters to Lady Elgin, 22 December 1857 and 12 June 1858, as cited in Theodore Walrond, *Letters and Journals of James, Eighth Earl of Elgin* (London: J. Murray, 1872), pp. 212–213 and 252–253.

9. Lord Elgin, as cited in J. L. Morison, *The Eighth Earl of Elgin* (London: Hodder and Stoughton, 1928), pp. 202, 258; and George Wrong, *The Earl of Elgin* (London: Methuen, 1905), p. 105.

10. Lord Elgin, as cited in Nathan A. Pelcovits, *Old China Hands and the Foreign Office* (New York: King's Crown Press, 1948), p. 18.

11. Lord Elgin, as cited in Walrond, *Letters and Journals,* p. 305. Elgin knew whereof he spoke, having reduced the Chinese emperor's Summer Palace to ashes in August 1860, during his occupation of Peking.

12. Lord Stanley, as cited in Pelcovits, *Old China Hands,* p. 38.

13. Ibid., p. 58.

14. Parker's career, including both missionary and diplomatic phases, is traced in Edward V. Gulick, *Peter Parker and the Opening of China* (Cambridge: Harvard University Press, 1973).

15. Te-kong Tong, *United States Diplomacy in China, 1844–1860* (Seattle: University of Washington Press, 1964), pp. 173–174.

16. W. C. Costin, *Great Britain and China 1833–1860* (Oxford: The Clarendon Press, 1937), p. 195.

17. Tong, *United States Diplomacy in China,* p. 195.

18. Ibid., pp. 203–206.

19. J. M. Callahan, *American Relations in the Pacific and the Far East, 1784–1900,* Johns Hopkins University Studies in Historical and Political Science, ser. 19, nos. 1–3 (Baltimore: The Johns Hopkins Press, 1901), p. 98.

20. J. W. Foster, *American Diplomacy in the Orient* (Boston and New York: Houghton, Mifflin and Co.; The Riverside Press, Cambridge, 1903), pp. 227–228.

21. Tong, *United States Diplomacy in China,* p. 196.

22. Ibid., p. 199.

23. Ibid., p. 200.

24. S. F. Bemis (ed.), *The American Secretaries of State and Their Diplomacy*, vols. 5–6 (New York: Pageant Book Co., 1958), p. 375.

25. Paul H. Clyde, *United States Policy Toward China: Diplomatic and Public Documents, 1839–1939* (New York: Russell and Russell, 1940), p. 40.

26. For more discussion on this point, see Immanuel C.Y. Hsu, *China's Entrance into the Family of Nations: The Diplomatic Phase, 1858–1880* (Cambridge: Harvard University Press, 1960).

27. One of the best sources on the role of Soviet advisers during the 1920s is C. Martin Wilbur and Julie Lien-ying How (eds.), *Documents on Communism, Nationalism, and Soviet Advisers in China, 1918–1927* (New York: Columbia University Press, 1956).

28. For a detailed account of Borodin's role in China during this period, see Dan N. Jacobs, *Borodin: Stalin's Man in China* (Cambridge: Harvard University Press, 1981).

29. Roy, a Hindu Brahmin by birth, was the Comintern's most prominent Marxist theoretician for Asia. His role in China is treated in Robert C. North and Xenia J. Eudin, *M. N. Roy's Mission to China: The Communist-Kuomintang Split of 1927* (New York: Octagon Books, 1977).

30. Dan N. Jacobs, "Soviet Russia and Chinese Nationalism in the 1920's," in Gilbert Chan and Thomas H. Etzold (eds.), *China in the 1920s* (New York: New Viewpoints, 1976), p. 51.

31. Dan N. Jacobs, "Recent Russian Material on Soviet Advisers in China: 1923–27," *China Quarterly* 41 (January–March, 1970), p. 103.

32. Ibid., pp. 106–107. Kazanin was not alone. For an extensive list of other Soviet sinologists who were in China during the period 1925–1927 and who suffered "Stalinist repression" in the 1930s, see the memoirs of one of the survivors: Vera Vladimirovna Vishnyakova-Akimova, *Two Years in Revolutionary China, 1925–27*, Steven I. Levine (trans.) (Cambridge: East Asian Research Center, Harvard University, 1971) pp. 30–31.

33. Vishnyakova-Akimova, *Two Years*, p. viii.

34. Jacobs, "Soviet Russia and Chinese Nationalism," p. 41.

35. One individual who comes to mind in this regard is Joseph Needham, the distinguished scientist-sinologist who served as head of the British Scientific Mission in China and counsellor, British Embassy, Chungking, during the 1942–1946 period.

36. British policy during this period is treated in Aron Shai, *Britain and China: 1941–1947* (New York: St. Martin's Press, 1984).

37. Mao Tse-tung, "Farewell, Leighton Stuart!" (August 18, 1949), *Selected Works of Mao Tse-tung*, vol. 4 (Peking: Foreign Languages Press, 1975), pp. 433, 439.

AKIRA IRIYE

4

The China Hands in History:
American Diplomacy in Asia

The China Hands present one of the most fascinating and instructive cases of modern history. In the first instance, of course, the experiences of individual diplomats like John Paton Davies and John F. Melby and journalists like John W. Powell greatly illuminate many of the motivations and practices of American diplomacy in the Far East. But in addition, their lives and careers, and those of their colleagues, provide a unique look at that precise point in time when American history and Chinese history intersected in important and fundamental ways. Even more, the experiences of the China Hands tell us about much more than the history of America, or the history of China, or of Chinese-American relations: They involve issues that cross national boundaries, that consider the world as a whole, and that address us today. Not the least of these is the important subject of ethics and diplomacy.

I would like to begin my discussion of China, strangely enough, with reference to Europe. Two years ago I attended a symposium on George Orwell's novel, *1984*, in Strasbourg, France, the seat of the Council of Europe. Although at first sight such a session may appear to have little to do with American-Chinese relations, and in fact China was hardly mentioned during the three-day conference, it soon became apparent to me that certain problems transcended geographical and cultural boundaries and that what Europeans discussed among themselves was just as relevant to Americans, Chinese, and all others. For Europeans who have experienced the

Stalinist dictatorship, Nazi concentration camps, and the destructive wars of the recent past, Orwell's depiction of a totalitarian dictatorship in a constant state of war preparedness is more than a literary caricature—it conveys a sense of reality. For this very reason, those I met at the Strasbourg symposium appeared proud of the fact that Europeans had not waged war against one another for nearly forty years now and that freedom and human rights had been preserved through their determined and united efforts. At the same time, many of them insisted that peace in Europe would be insecure until there was global stability and that freedom was indivisible and ought to be safeguarded regardless of national differences.

All these ideas, it seems to me, are relevant to our discussion of American-Chinese relations. In this chapter I shall focus on four broad themes, all inspired by our current interest in Orwell, and try to relate them to the main subject of this book, that is, the experiences of the China Hands. These four themes are war and peace, memory and historical consciousness, utopianism and the modern state, and intercultural communication and understanding. These problems occupy central positions in the annals of American-Chinese relations; they are also linked to the important question of ethics and public service.

War and Peace

First of all, Orwell's novel depicts a world consisting of three large empires that are in a perpetual state of tension and potential conflict. Their governments are all totalitarian regimes and their people submissive automatons without freedom or individuality. They do not know each other well, but actually there is little point in trying to do so because they are all alike. Each state is characterized by total mobilization for war, which is the only way the rulers can keep the masses under control. All products of modern technology and political organization are utilized to perpetuate a totalitarian system in which power becomes its own end. The state of American-Chinese relations after 1949 until the early 1970s, as John Melby discusses in Chapter 6, at least partially corresponded to Orwell's description of mutual hostility and almost total absence of communication between two countries. What was so poignant about this was that for many years prior to 1949 Americans and Chinese had been accustomed to viewing their relationship as something very special, a unique instance of friendship and interdependence. Then almost overnight they found themselves engulfed in campaigns of mutual hatred, as if they had to eradicate all memories of the past. The United States came to justify its involvement in Asian wars by linking them to the overall objective of containing Chinese power, and the People's Republic of China sought to undermine American hegemony by inciting anti-American movements throughout the world. Yet, there was no direct military confrontation between the two countries, at least after the Korean War. This was a condition of neither war nor peace or, rather, peace defined as war preparedness. Then, just as suddenly, in the early 1970s, the United States and China effected a rapprochement to balance the growing power of the Soviet Union, precisely as had been predicted by George Orwell. The two peoples were now encouraged to recall, once again, their traditional friendship and to resume their contact.

What underlay such shifts and turns in American-Chinese relations were, in the words of Henry Kissinger, "the geopolitical realities of the world"—in other words, power politics. Kissinger and other so-called "realists" have written that the American people have never learned to accept geopolitics but have tended to indulge in parochial and sentimental notions about foreign affairs. These critics, in my view, have exaggerated the parochialism and sentimentalism underlying American relations with the rest of the world. After all, there exists, going all the way back to Alexander Hamilton and George Washington, a realistic tradition that stresses the importance of power considerations in diplomacy. This tradition was reinforced at the turn of the twentieth century when leaders such as Theodore Roosevelt and Woodrow Wilson defined the United States as a world power and sought to make use of the nation's military and economic power to influence the politics of other countries and to establish a stable international order. This will to power was weakened considerably during the prosperous decade of the 1920s, when it seemed as if a "war to end all wars" had just been fought, and in the Depression decade of the 1930s, when the best strategy for economic salvation appeared to lie in isolating the country from world affairs. But then, from around 1940, a new awareness of the importance of power emerged in the face of the aggressive policies of Germany, Japan, and the Soviet Union. It became incumbent upon the United States to reenter world politics, expand its armament, and ally itself with others who would defend the status quo. Americans, it may be said, self-consciously embraced power politics in the belief, as a *New Republic* editorial noted in 1941, that "if a democracy is not prepared to be militant, it is not prepared to survive."

This view, that national survival necessitated a policy based on power considerations, justified an alliance with a totalitarian Russia against a totalitarian Germany and Japan, just as it would impel the United States a few years afterward to enter into an alliance with Germany and Japan against the Soviet Union. Similarly, American strategy in the Pacific at first called for the use of China as a deterrent to Japanese power, which was subsequently followed by a policy of arming Japan to contain Chinese power. All these developments bear out George Washington's assertion in his famous Farewell Address almost two centuries ago that in power politics, there are no permanent friends or permanent enemies. By the same token, China has been a practitioner of power politics, as have other countries. In fact, this is what is most disconcerting about the contemporary world. All nations, large and small, are armed to the teeth, delight in militant diplomacy, engage in deceptive strategies, and collectively contribute to bringing mankind a step closer to its extinction.

The China Hands, like other officials and private citizens, were caught in the maelstrom of shifting power realities. It is not that they were too naive to understand the power factor in international affairs. On the contrary, they strongly believed in building China up as a power against Japan so that with America it would be able to maintain a stable Asian order. Some of the China Hands, moreover, believed in checking the growth of Soviet power in Asia through forming close ties between Americans and Chinese Communists. It was ironic that their advocacy of a balance of power strategy ran afoul of an official policy that assumed a basic power rivalry between the United States and China. The point is, however, that in a world in which geopolitical strategies and Machiavellian tactics are commonplace, officials who advocate a certain approach may gain temporary recognition, only to be forgotten when the government defines a new position.

This may be the usual fate of all diplomats. The case of America's China Hands indicates, however, another important fact—namely, that power politics not only determines relations among states but also affects domestic politics. In the name of pursuing geopolitical objectives abroad, the state often seeks to augment its own power at home. This entails the ascendancy of the military in decision-making, censorship and other kinds of control of information, and domestic surveillance of citizens. These phenomena have characterized all modern powers, including, if to a lesser extent than other countries, the United States, where the National Security Act established the basic framework for waging the Cold War as early as 1947. The Federal Employee Loyalty Program was one product of the concern with security, as were other measures designed to test officials' loyalty to the state. In the prevailing atmosphere of Cold War tensions, the augmentation of military power abroad and the power of the state at home was widely accepted as necessary.

It was not surprising that the China Hands—those who were knowledgeable about China and sought to promote close relations between the two countries—were among the first casualties of this state of affairs. They became victims of the Cold War in two respects. First, when abroad, their advocacy of friendly ties with China was no longer in accord with official policy. The United States was now dealing with a country whose Maoist leadership talked of "permanent war" so that America would have to respond in kind. Second, at home, pro-Chinese spokesmen were accused of disloyalty. It was as if those diplomats and journalists who had established ties with Chinese Communists had been contaminated with evil, so that their services would no longer be desirable.

Memory and Historical Consciousness

In the subsequent ordeal of the China Hands, perhaps the most terrifying aspect concerned the problem of memory and historical consciousness. This is the second theme I wish to discuss. As Orwell described it so well, "who controls the past controls the future; who controls the present controls the past." Those who came to dominate American politics and policy in the early Cold War years should not be equated with more extreme dictators. But they nevertheless showed an extreme sensitivity about the recent past and, in the process, attested to the Orwellian dictum that memory is the first casualty of arbitrary government. One could generalize and say that freedom to remember is perhaps the most precious of human rights; without memory there can be no individuality, no personality; and without such freedom there exists no community, and therefore no civilization. Culture, as Lewis Mumford has said, is accumulated human memory. History, we may add, is a past freely remembered, so that culture and history are obliterated once memory is suppressed, distorted, or manipulated at the whim of the state.

Although the harrassment and humiliation of many China Hands never reached Orwellian proportions, nevertheless it is illuminating that they were subjected to constant interrogations, public and private, during which they were to explain the past, to say they had committed a grave error, or to admit they had aided the enemy of the United States. The state defined the only framework in which a diplomat's or journalist's past record could be evaluated, and reports were taken out of context to fit a distorted history that was more convenient to the state's needs. What was so unfortunate was that such rewriting of history was a standard practice of totalitarian dictatorships, the very countries against which the United States was supposedly engaged in a Cold War to preserve freedom. There was a profound irony in waging a war for freedom by striking a blow against human memory. The inquisitions of the China Hands were justified on the grounds that the Cold War had to be waged by all means, not just military and economic but cultural and ideological, and therefore it was necessary to ensure mobilization of citizens' minds as well as material resources. Mobilization of historical consciousness was an aspect of this endeavor, but by definition it entailed manipulation of the past. To their credit, the China Hands did not succumb to such rewriting of history, and thus, it may be said, contributed in the long run to preserving the legacy of freedom.

I have dwelt on aspects of the China Hands' experience that show how even in a democratic society the state of perpetual war preparedness could do damage to freedom by striking at the most precious gift of memory. Although today the honor and reputation of the former diplomats have been restored, there is no assurance that another assault on historical consciousness will not take place. Moreover, in many countries today state control over history continues. Those in power choose past events that they want emphasized in educating the masses. Just as the Chinese people were told in the 1950s and the 1960s to remember the evils of American imperialism, for example, now they are given a picture of the traditional friendship between the two peoples. Chinese historians who have sought to go beyond such simplistic ideas have found it extremely difficult to reconstruct a past that corresponds to the evidence. So long as global tensions continue, and so long as the Chinese leadership places a premium on military preparedness, whether against the Soviet Union or other countries, tight control over historical consciousness will be maintained. The ordeal and legacy of the China Hands are a reminder that there are enormous obstacles in the way of freedom in a world in which organized mass states vie with one another for greater power.

Utopianism and the Modern State

The story of American-Chinese relations and of the China Hands is not, however, merely one of war preparedness or arbitrary shifts and turns in power politics. In the long run, the significance of the China Hands may be their exemplification of what I would call the role of the American reformist tradition in the building of new nations. This is the third theme that I wish to discuss, at somewhat greater length than the others because it is central to understanding the history of American foreign relations. An important characteristic of the United States is that it is the first modern state built on utopian aspirations that have not led to extreme forms of social engineering or dictatorships of the right or the left. For those who have experienced the Nazi concentration camps, Soviet gulags, or Chinese cultural revolutions, utopianism is nothing but a nightmare—a product of man's hubristic attempts to create a perfect world. In modern states, the elite has made use of advanced technology to indulge in social and biological experimentation, with the consequent loss of individual freedom. The combination of will to power, technology, and ideology is what sustains an Orwellian state.

In the United States, too, utopianism has entailed visions of technological advancement in the service of ideas. Unlike utopianism in many other societies, however, American utopianism has taken the form of secular reform, or liberalism, the term often used. American reformism was characterized by two features that revealed a rather pragmatic agenda. One was its emphasis on evolutionary, as opposed to revolutionary, change. Reformism implied man's ability to modify his surroundings through patient efforts rather than through violent upheaval. More specifically, it assumed that technological progress and economic development would be matched by the evolution of political institutions that would serve the rights and interests of all citizens. The stress here was not on effecting a wholesale transformation of society or of man, but on institutional adjustments. The second characteristic was that reform at home was seen as interdependent with reform abroad. The resulting symbiotic relationship meant that the betterment of the human condition in the world hinged on progress in America, and vice versa. Such a view encouraged an attitude toward foreign affairs that was at once nationalistic and internationalist. In fact, nationalism and internationalism were both sides of the same coin. Promoting America's national interest was considered the same thing as working for a better world order. Conversely, as Woodrow Wilson said, American interests could be protected only if conditions of freedom, justice, and economic advancement prevailed throughout the world.

These reformist ideas were as relevant to the history of American relations with China as power considerations. It is no accident that the so-called age of reform in the United States, namely the Progressive Era from the turn of the twentieth century through World War I, coincided with a burst of interest in Chinese affairs. American religious, business, legal, and academic leaders who constituted the core of the Progressive movement were also attracted to the prospect of encouraging reform in China. It is not surprising that given their reformist orientation, they found a great deal to admire both in the efforts of the late Ch'ing dynasty to undertake last-minute reforms and in the attempts of the early Republic which came into existence in 1912, to initiate economic and political modernization. It seemed axiomatic that America would serve as an excellent model for the Chinese, not simply in its political institutions but in its educational and economic systems as well. The stress was not on radical or revolutionary change, but gradualist transformation, as can be seen in the support given Yuan Shih-k'ai when he emerged as the leader of the country. At the same time, American reformers believed that their domestic agenda would benefit if changes took place in China. A successful endeavor overseas would be a sign that reformism was still viable at home. Together America and China, and all other countries similarly inspired, would promote a more interdependent, prosperous, and peaceful world order.

The China Hands, it seems to me, were heirs to this reformist tradition. Of course, this is not the only tradition they inherited. As I suggested earlier, concern with power considerations was always an influential factor, but reformist ideas gave American diplomacy its unique character. What happened in the twentieth century, particularly under the presidency of Woodrow Wilson, was that power was placed at the service of ideas so that the United States used its massive military power in Latin America and Europe in order to help modernize traditional societies. American diplomats were keenly aware of power-political factors in international affairs, but they also shared with their countrymen a belief in broader tasks their nation seemed to carry in dealing with other countries. These tasks were particularly well defined for underdeveloped countries such as China, which went through a long period of turmoil following World War I.

It was precisely in the years after World War I that the China Hands made their debut. They entered the Foreign Service, or the journalistic or academic professions, and were stationed in various parts of China in the 1920s and 1930s, a period of domestic strife and foreign aggression in China unparalleled in modern Asian history. We should not lose sight of the central drama, however—namely, the establishment of a modern Chinese state that had received its inspiration from the May Fourth Movement, developed from a major nationalistic movement in the 1920s, and suffered from the world economic crisis of the 1930s, which abetted Japanese expansionism. Such a country was a perfect candidate to receive the gifts extended from America's helping hand. American missionaries, journalists, educators, and diplomats were impressed and encouraged by the efforts of the Chinese to found a centralized government and to undertake economic modernization. At the end of the 1920s, when the Nationalist government was established, the United States was quick to recognize it and to negotiate with it for revision of the unequal treaties. Economic and technical assistance programs were undertaken by private individuals, church groups, and foundations. All these endeavors fitted the framework of American reformism, the thrust of which was to help what would later be called "nation-building" efforts by an underdeveloped country. Like subsequent attempts, nation-building in China was characterized by the development of an infrastructure to facilitate economic modernization, the emergence of an elite corps of bureaucrats and technologists with close connections to America, and the creation of a political apparatus to enable the country to become a force in international affairs. There is little doubt that American diplomats and others in China supported these programs wholeheartedly.

Unfortunately, their impact, and American influence in China generally, declined in the 1930s because of the Depression. This was one period when reform at home was not accompanied by an active reformist agenda abroad. One consequence of America's minimal involvement in overseas affairs in the 1930s was China's isolation in world politics—a result best seen in China's failure to obtain Western support against Japan during the Manchurian crisis. In a sense, the growing intensity of the Kuomintang-Communist struggle for power reflected these developments. On one hand, the Communists presented themselves as more nationalistic than the Nationalists in China's resistance to Japanese aggression. Since little foreign support was forthcoming, the Communists emerged as the focal point of the coalescing nationalistic sentiment. At the same time, the reduction in American-initiated reform programs highlighted the fact that the Communists were more willing than the Nationalists to emerge as advocates of domestic reform. The idea of the Communists as reformers as well as nationalists was in sharp contrast to the spectacle of Nationalists turning to Germany for military advice and ideological inspiration.

There was another twist in the late 1930s as factions in China came together to form a united front against Japan and as Western powers eventually came to incorporate China into their global strategies. In many ways the years between 1937 and 1945 marked a decisive stage in the formation of the modern Chinese state. Although much of the country was occupied by Japanese troops, and industrial and cultural institutions were removed from coastal cities to the hinterland, the war was expected ultimately to bring about China's emergence as a sovereign state. War needs and the infusion of foreign, particularly American, aid would impel China to modernize its institutions. It would become more closely linked to the world economy. Such, at least, were the prevailing perceptions in China as well as elsewhere. Americans, in particular, took for granted that after the war they would have in China a reliable, modern partner with whom they would be able to cooperate in creating a more stable Asia.

It was, however, also during the war that American officials developed a serious division of views as to Chinese politics. In our context, the dispute was over which of the Chinese factions was the best candidate to be the force for a modern state. Put another way, the issue was which individuals and groups deserved American support, and here American support followed reformist tradition so that the United States would assist those forces and movements in China that promoted the country's unification, independence, and reform. Independence would mean not only liberation from Japanese aggression but also freedom from external domination such as Soviet communism and British imperialism. Independence, however, would not mean China's isolation from the world. On the contrary, it would entail its linkage, economically and politically, to the rest of the globe so that China, as the world's most populous country, would be able to become a spokesman for human aspirations everywhere. Such was the reformist agenda as developed by American officials, and it was defined in very traditional terms. What was perceived was an image of China that would share certain values with American liberalism and that would replicate the reformist features of American democracy. For many of the China Hands, the Communists appeared in this regard to be more deserving of support than the Nationalists, whereas for some others, the latter were truer to American ideals. But the essential fact to remember is that both sides took it for granted that China would develop as a modern state after the war, linked closely to the United States and to the rest of the world.

The debate as to which factions in China represented the best hope for the country and for the United States might have remained purely academic but for the fact that American reformism encountered an unprecedented challenge after 1945 in the form of Soviet military power and political totalitarianism. Whatever crises American democracy and reformism had experienced in the past had been generated domestically. Now, however, the crisis was from an external source: For the first time the Soviet Union was in control of most of the neighboring states, reestablishing a tight police system, and launching a five-year plan in preparation for war, as Stalin declared in 1946. Should China fall into the Soviet orbit, much of the Eurasian continent would be closed to outside contact and, worse, pose a threat to the global balance of power. At this juncture, power considerations began to overshadow reformist precepts. Of critical importance now was not so much whether China would be democratic and reformist, but whether it would remain tied to the United States in the global struggle for power. Recent studies have revealed that some of the high officials of the Truman administration were at first seriously interested in the possibility of detaching the People's Republic of China from Soviet influence. This was essentially a power-political approach, little related to an evaluation of the nature of Chinese politics, but it seemed wise to keep Communist China and Communist Russia from combining to create a gigantic bloc. When such an attempt failed, as became clear when the two communist countries signed a treaty of friendship and alliance in early 1950, the United States' reaction was predictable. Believing that China had been lost to the Soviet sphere, Americans began attacking their officials who had failed to prevent the development.

Thus the ordeal of the China Hands may be better understood by placing it against the historical background that I have tried to sketch. In the context of China's nation-making efforts and America's reformist response to them, the China Hands were loyal representatives of their country's legacy. They *had* contributed to the emergence of a modern Chinese state, whether Nationalist or Communist. It was their misfortune that just at the moment when their contributions should have been crowned with success and accolade, American-Chinese relations became dominated by the power-political equation that was pitting the United States against the Soviet Union. Yet in the long run, the Sino-Soviet connection proved short-lived, certainly of much shorter duration than the nation-building efforts by the Chinese. Today, when the Chinese leadership is once again acknowledging the need for American assistance as they undertake modernization programs, the China Hands may feel vindicated. In the long history of U.S.-Chinese relations, their ordeal in the 1950s, even though a tragedy in human terms, was but a brief interlude. Their contributions are as enduring as American reformism.

Intercultural Communication and Understanding

This having been said, we must go farther and ask whether the American reformist legacy equips this country to deal effectively with other countries, particularly those of the Third World. Ultimately, our evaluation of the China Hands' contributions to history, and of the history of American-Chinese relations, must lead to questions about intercultural understanding and communication. This is the fourth and last theme in this chapter. American reformism envisaged a utopia of technological advancement, economic development, educational modernization, and political change. Has this been, or will it continue to be, a viable agenda for the rest of the world? Of these ingredients of reform, technological and economic change is more tangible and probably less controversial. All countries, even including those hostile to the United States, appear to have been eager to borrow American technology and obtain American capital. The intangibles of education, political ideology, and mentality—in short, cultural orientations—are what are open to debate.

Yet it is clear that the reformist tradition in America had, from its inception, cultural objectives. It aimed at educating other peoples, inculcating in them ideas of liberty, and opening their minds to vistas of progress and enlightenment. These were considered crucial in creating a network of individuals throughout the world who would have similar orientations and thus contribute to international harmony and peace. One specific manifestation of this in American-Chinese relations was the education of Chinese youth in American schools, both in the United States and in China. For example in the 1920s when China was hardly significant to American security, and when trade between the two countries was minimal, 1,000 or more Chinese came to the United States annually to study at institutions of higher learning. They were by far the most numerous group of foreign students and indicated the crucial role played by nonmilitary, non-economic issues in American-Chinese relations. These Chinese were agents of cultural transfer, and through their efforts it was expected that Chinese society would be subtly and steadily transformed. Of course, one could question whether Chinese students who came to the United States really appreciated American values, or whether, upon their return, they contributed to the promotion of liberty and intellectual freedom in their own country. Moreover, cultural contact does not in itself ensure friendly diplomatic relations. China and Japan, after all, maintained far more extensive cultural ties than China and the United States, but that did not prevent Japanese aggression in China or the development of profound mutual hostility between those two peoples.

Rather, the crucial point is that cultural relations cannot be undertaken without the efforts of individuals to function as intermediaries or as communicators. To the extent that communication is a fundamental requirement for conducting international affairs, one has to turn to individuals who are intellectually and psychologically equipped to do the communicating. It is a two-way art, consisting of learning from another culture while teaching one's own.

The role of the China Hands as communicators thus becomes quite clear. Some of them were born in China, and most of them knew the language well. They not only encouraged the Chinese they met to appreciate certain American values, but also tried to interpret Chinese perspectives to Americans. They, together with some journalists and scholars, contributed to making American-Chinese relations more of an intellectual exchange. Their efforts as intermediary communicators, to be sure, often ended in frustration. During the McCarthy Era, they were accused of having been naive in applying the vocabulary of Western liberal democracy to a country without a similar tradition. They were particularly criticized for not having studied Marxism and Leninism as ideological foundations of the Chinese Communist movement. Similar accusations have been made, ironically, by America's social scientists and radical historians who emphasize the role of ideology in human behavior. In a sense, many of the China Hands represented the old-fashioned humanist tradition, assuming that one could promote mutual understanding through personal contact. There is no easy way to international understanding, but at least it would appear that when the dust settled, after the turmoil of the 1950s and the 1960s, what was most impressive about American-Chinese relations was the resumption of personal friendships and associations that had been interrupted for three decades. The American diplomats who went back to China to a warm welcome after years of separation were proof that cultural contact endures and is more durable than constantly changing power relations.

I mentioned at the outset the Council of Europe, which was established in 1949 to preserve the precious heritages of freedom, democracy, and human rights in the West. Its member countries shared these values, derived from a common Judeo-Christian tradition. Whether there could be a counterpart to the Council of Europe in other parts of the world is a fascinating question. One could argue that some American diplomats in China before the war genuinely believed it was possible to develop a special relationship between the two countries on the basis of shared values and aspirations. It is easy to be cynical about such views, but the idea that the two countries' relations should be built on more than just geopolitical needs should not be cavalierly dismissed, for enough evidence indicates that individual Chinese today aspire to some of the same objectives as individual Americans. Moreover, Americans today, compared to a generation ago, appear to be more open-minded and tolerant of diversity in the world than their forefathers. They are less likely to condemn another country simply because it is socialist. Such broad-mindedness, if maintained, will make it possible for the two countries to work together in cultural matters. In both these regards—that is, in pointing to areas of shared aspirations and in being open-minded about another cultural tradition—many of the China Hands may be said to have made an important contribution to crosscultural understanding.

To conclude, the legacy of the China Hands illuminates the promise and frustrations in the history of American-Chinese relations. This history, I have tried to argue, must be comprehended at many levels: power rivalries, modernization, crosscultural interchange. Yet ultimately, like everything else, it may be a matter of individual personality, faith, and ethics. There may be a gap, a serious one as we know from the experiences of the China Hands, between a diplomat as a public servant and as a private person. Between these two poles, there may be a third level of existential identification, namely, a membership in a community of civilized human beings, an invisible bond that connects those who would communicate with one another openly and freely across national boundaries. The future of the world and of freedom may hinge on this group of individuals, those that the novelist E. M. Forster called "an aristocracy of the sensitive, the considerate, and the plucky." The China Hands would seem to have proven the existence of such an aristocracy.

For Further Reading

Readers interested in learning more about the experiences of China Hands will benefit from an excellent study of an American diplomat: Gary May's *China Scapegoat: The Ordeal of John Carter Vincent* (Washington, D.C.: New Republic Books, 1979). For a broader discussion of American diplomats' roles in China during the 1930s and the 1940s, consult James C. Thomson, *While China Faced West* (Cambridge: Harvard University Press, 1969) and Michael Schaller, *The U.S. Crusade in China* (New York: Columbia University Press, 1979). The evolution of postwar U.S.-Chinese relations is described in great detail in Nancy B. Tucker, *Patterns in the Dust* (New York: Columbia University Press, 1983). The themes of liberal reformism and cultural internationalism that are developed in the essay are well presented in such books as Emily Rosenberg, *Spreading the American Dream* (New York: Hill and Wang, 1982); Frank Ninkovich, *The Diplomacy of Ideas* (Cambridge: Cambridge University Press, 1982); and Robert Packenham, *American Liberalism and the Third World* (Princeton: Princeton University Press, 1973). Among the most recent analyses of Nationalist Chinese politics and ideology are Lloyd Eastman, *Seeds of Destruction: Nationalist China in War and Revolution* (Stanford: Stanford University Press, 1984), and William Kirby, *Germany and Republican China* (Stanford: Stanford University Press, 1984). Finally, my discussion of Orwellianism and liberalism has been inspired by E. M. Forster, *Two Cheers for Democracy* (New York: Harcourt, 1951), and by various essays included in Nobutoshi Hagihara et al. (eds.), *Experiencing the Twentieth Century* (Tokyo: University of Tokyo Press, 1985).

ERNEST R. MAY

5

The China Hands In Perspective: Ethics, Diplomacy, and Statecraft

Of the State Department China Hands, Theodore White writes in *In Search of History*:

> It was Lord Acton who, in his inaugural lecture at Cambridge on the study of history a century ago, said: "I exhort you never . . . to lower the standard of rectitude . . . to suffer no man and no cause to escape the undying penalty which history has the power to inflict on wrong." The wrong done by the McCarthy lancers, under McCarthy leadership, was to poke out the eyes and ears of the State Department on Asian affairs, to blind American foreign policy. And thus flying blind into the murk of Asian politics, American diplomacy carried American honor, resources, and lives into the triple canopied jungles and green-carpeted hills of Vietnam where all crashed.[1]

The propositions, implicit or explicit, in this statement by White (stated less poetically and less eloquently by others) are that it was clearly wrong for the government to have fired the China Hands and that if the China Hands had been present in the government, then the wrong decisions with regard to Vietnam would not have been made. I would like to suggest that we look again at these propositions and consider if, indeed, the people who had to make choices did not view them as moral decisions. That is, that the people who made the decisions to dismiss the China Hands—

Secretary of State Dean Acheson and Secretary of State John Foster Dulles—may have been doing what they thought to be right, morally right, in making ethical choices. And, likewise, that President Lyndon Johnson years later—when he made the critical commitment of American forces to Vietnam—similarly may have felt, with some basis, that he was making a moral choice, a diplomatic decision on ethical grounds. If we think about those issues as they presented themselves to the people who had to decide them, in ethical as well as practical terms, and if we had been in their places, or indeed even if the China Hands themselves had been in their places having to make decisions with their responsibilities, the choices might well have been the same.

Most American intellectuals probably agree with White that the firing of the China Hands was unconscionable and that a lack of the China Hands' feel for Asia helped lead to Vietnam. Both propositions are open to question. White simplifies by blaming McCarthy. Actually, the man who purged the China Hands was Dean Acheson. In the same period, Acheson went out of his way to say that he would not turn his back on Alger Hiss, just convicted of perjury (and, in most minds, of spying). Explaining his motive, Acheson said to a hostile congressional committee:

> One must be true to the things by which one lives. The counsels of discretion and cowardice are appealing. The safe course is to avoid situations which are disagreeable and dangerous. Such a course might get one by the issue of the moment, but it has bitter and evil consequences. In the long days and years which stretch beyond that moment of decision, one must live with one's self; and the consequences of living with a decision which one knows has sprung from timidity and cowardice go to the roots of one's life. It is not merely a question of peace of mind, although that is vital; it is a matter of integrity of character.[2]

One cannot explain Acheson's actions regarding the China Hands as an example of a wicked man doing a wicked thing.

Nor does a close look at the evidence help make a case that Vietnam policy would have been different if China Hands had had a voice in it. The more we learn about the period, the more it seems that people in Washington understood what was happening in Asia. It was America they misinterpreted, not Vietnam.

Purging the China Hands

Let me start with the purge of the China Hands.[3] Attention in this area is generally focused upon Dulles, but it must be remembered that the purge actually began before Acheson was secretary of state—in the days when he was under secretary, first for James F. Byrnes and then for George C. Marshall. The *Amerasia* case, breaking in the spring of 1945, set it off. On the premises of that small-circulation, left-wing monthly, FBI agents seized a number of security-classified government documents. Some had been given the publisher by John Stewart Service, a middle-grade Foreign Service officer recently returned from China. A grand jury voted indictments against the publisher and some others, but not against Service. The jurors accepted his explanation that he had just provided background material to a seemingly legitimate journalist. The inadmissibility of some evidence illegally obtained complicated the proceeding. However, a State Department personnel board also cleared Service of wrongdoing.[4]

In November 1945, Patrick J. Hurley resigned as ambassador to China.[5] He told a congressional committee that careerists sympathetic to the Communists had subverted his efforts to support Chiang Kai-shek. He named Service, George Atcheson (no relation to Dean), John Paton Davies, Fulton Freeman, Arthur Ringwalt, John K. Emmerson, and John Carter Vincent. Though the legal adviser of the State Department pronounced the charges groundless, congressional committees repeatedly revived them. The State Department sent China Hands to posts away from Chinese affairs—Service to New Zealand and Vincent to Switzerland. Effectively manager of the department at that time, Acheson was responsible for their transfers.

When Acheson returned in 1949 to be secretary of state, Hurley's accusations still occupied congressional committees and State Department review boards. Jack Service was brought back to Washington in a routine administrative assignment so that he could undergo yet another round of hearings. A department board cleared him again. He was assigned to India, then reassigned as a result of congressional and press complaints, then by early 1950 was back in Washington doing what he characterized as "snake farm duty." During 1950 and 1951 he underwent investigation three more times, on the last occasion at the hands of a Loyalty Review Board commissioned by President Truman to stand outside and above the departments and to apply the test of whether there was "reasonable doubt as to . . . loyalty to the Government of the United States." This board ruled that Service's conduct in the *Amerasia* case provided basis for "reasonable doubt." Presented with this ruling, Acheson acted in a matter of hours, notifying Service that his discharge from the Foreign Service would take effect immediately.[6]

The process of separating the China Hands from any duty connected with China resumed. Raymond Ludden went to a series of consular posts in Europe, grumbling later that he "was just putting in . . . time." John Paton Davies was assigned first to the staff of the high commissioner for Germany and then to Peru. Fulton Freeman was sent to Rome.[7]

At about the same time of Service's firing, the various departmental and presidential review boards completed hearings on Oliver Clubb. Though they cleared him, he subsequently received an assignment that he judged to be the equivalent of a death sentence for a Foreign Service officer. (He was assigned to the Division of Historical Research.) Consequently, he resigned.[8]

John Carter Vincent, who had been minister to Switzerland, was demoted to consul general in Tangier. That post did not require Senate confirmation. Still, Congressional committees repeatedly questioned his fitness. Late in 1952, the same presidential Loyalty Board that had ruled against Service delivered a similar verdict against Vincent. By a 3–2 vote, it held that there was "reasonable doubt" as to his loyalty, the basis being his "studied praise of Chinese Communists and equally studied criticism of the Chiang Kai-shek government during a period when it was the declared and established policy of the Government of the United States to support Chiang Kai-shek's Government."[9]

In Vincent's case, Acheson did not act as expeditiously as with Service. He had worked with Vincent during the war and in testimony called him "a disinterested and loyal servant of our republic . . . [and] a man of the finest intellectual quality and the highest character."[10] Acheson asked Judge Learned Hand to head a special panel to take yet another look at the evidence. Having only weeks left in office, Acheson proposed that Hand's panel make its report to his successor. To Acheson's regret, but surely not to his surprise, John Foster Dulles did not avail himself of the offer. Dulles called Vincent in and offered him a choice of being fired or voluntarily resigning. The second alternative would enable him to keep his pension. Vincent chose it. In later years he was frequently to tell the story of how, to his amazement and that of his lawyer, Dulles accepted his formal letter of resignation and then invited him to sit down and have a drink, explaining to the lawyer, "I want to use this opportunity to ask the Minister some questions about China. After all, he knows the situation there better than just about anybody."[11]

Dulles also acted against Davies. Here, Joe McCarthy did play a part. In a gesture demonstrating his independence of the new Republican administration, McCarthy cited Davies's continuance in the Foreign Service as evidence that "the Communist problem" persisted. Dulles's security chief, Scott McLeod, responded by re-opening hearings on Davies, applying a new standard set by President Eisenhower—that any individual's employment in the executive branch be "clearly consistent with national security." In the summer of 1954 a hearing board concluded that Davies's employment did not meet that test. In November Dulles fired him.[12]

Otherwise, however, Dulles did nothing to current or former members of the department's Chinese language service. The only veteran of that service still on assignment in Asia, Everett Drumright, was made consul general to Hong Kong and subsequently ambassador to the Nationalist government on Taiwan. Emmerson, Freeman, and others who had been targets of Hurley and his friends—James K. Penfield, Edward Rice, and Philip Sprouse—rose routinely within the ranks of the Foreign Service. They simply did not draw assignments related to Asia. Because Vincent and Davies had both also been detached for some years from the Asian services, Dulles's actions in their cases did not affect then-current reporting about that part of the world. If the State Department was blinded, as Theodore White says, the blame has to be Acheson's.

Why, then, did he do it?

Surely, one would be hard put to argue that he acted in pure self-interest. His private and social life would have been happier without newspaper stories, columns, cartoons, and cocktail and dinner party conversation suggesting that he was knuckling under to people whom he himself called "primitives." Concerning Vincent's assignment to Tangier, for example, the *Washington Post* said that Acheson had "toadied outrageously to McCarthyism."[13] Any suggestion that Acheson compromised his conscience in order to keep his job is simply preposterous. When Acheson offered to resign on account of the furor over his refusal to turn his back on Hiss, Truman reminded him that he, as vice president, had attended the funeral of former Kansas City boss, and former felon, Tom Pendergast; Truman said he understood and approved and absolutely would hear no word of resignation.[14] Harry Truman would never—*never*—have broken with Acheson for putting principle or personal loyalty ahead of other considerations.

Was it "political expediency"—an otherwise honorable man choosing what he regarded as a lesser evil? In part, perhaps. The potential price of political inexpediency was high. For the European Recovery Program, the North Atlantic Treaty Organization (NATO), the rebuilding of Germany and Japan, and other efforts that Acheson thought vitally important, the administration needed votes from senators and representatives who distrusted the China Hands. This fact must have carried some weight with Acheson.

One can argue, however, that Acheson was not compromising principle but instead reluctantly obeying it. Personally, he disdained most of these senators and representatives. Some he actually abhorred. Large numbers of other well-educated, cosmopolitan Americans felt as he did. Joe McCarthy, as John Melby correctly reminds us elsewhere in this volume, was simply the one whose name became a generic label. Styles Bridges of New Hampshire, Homer Capehart and William E. Jenner of Indiana, Bourke Hickenlooper of Iowa, Kenneth Wherry of Nebraska, and, on the House side, J. Parnell Thomas of New Jersey, Harold Velde of Illinois, Karl Mundt of North Dakota, and Richard Nixon of California behaved much as McCarthy did. But these men were elected representatives of the people. Moreover, after they had made their opinions notorious and after educated cosmopolites had had plenty of innings for rebuttal, voters emphatically renewed their mandates.[15]

The demand from the legislative branch did not issue just from a handful of publicity seekers. Robert A. Taft of Ohio, leader of Republicans in the Senate, member (along with Acheson) of the Yale Corporation, sometimes referred to as "Mr. Integrity," also said that he would not simply take the word of the secretary of state— or the president—that nothing was amiss. William F. Knowland of California, whom Senate Republicans would choose to be their new leader after Taft succumbed to cancer, was fervent on the point. Arthur Vandenberg of Michigan, chief proponent among Republicans of bipartisan cooperation on foreign policy, declared himself of similar mind. Indeed, no Republican who otherwise collaborated with the Truman administration on foreign affairs was prepared to vote confidence in its handling of the inquiries into the China Hands. Not Alexander Wiley of Wisconsin. Not Henry Cabot Lodge of Massachusetts. Not Margaret Chase Smith of Maine. A "declaration of conscience" signed in 1950 by Smith and other Senate Republicans merely condemned McCarthy's methods. It did not say that the administration's methods had produced unsatisfactory results. In any case, the signers of the declaration had counterweights across the aisle in, for example, Pat McCarran of Nevada and James Eastland of Mississippi, whose open mistrust of the administration matched that of any Republican.[16]

The fact cannot be ignored that Acheson had clear evidence of the legislative branch's desire that the State Department be purged of people who had advocated withdrawing support from Chiang. The 1980s saw something roughly similar. The legislative branch did not approve environmental policies associated with James Watt and Anne Gorsuch Burford. Misdeeds by Rita Lavelle, a political appointee in the Environmental Protection Administration, gave Congress the lever that the *Amerasia* affair and Hurley's charges had given the foes of the China Hands. It forced a purge. This time, educated, cosmopolitan Americans generally applauded. Clearly the parallel cannot be pushed far. The congressional critics of Watt and Burford did not behave like McCarthy or Jenner or McCarran. But the two cases have enough in common to make the point that our evolving constitutional system gives the legislative branch some power over executive personnel. In the late 1940s and early 1950s, the legislative branch exerted that power against the China Hands. It is not clear that, as a matter of either law or faith or morality,

Secretary Acheson had better cause to resist than did members of the Reagan administration thirty-odd years later.

A protest that the China Hands were punished for what they reported, not for what they advocated, would be ingenuous. There was no doubt that the China Hands opposed supporting Chiang. They believed that the facts they described ought to cause that policy to change. Not because of any ulterior connection or motive, but out of their judgment as to what would be best for everyone, some of them favored accommodation with the Chinese Communists. They may have been right on all these points. The policies they favored might well have been wiser policies. But elected representatives of the American people felt differently, and the China Hands became targets of attack because of the policies their reportage encouraged, not because their reportage was inaccurate. And that was exactly what more temperate members of Congress such as Vandenberg and Walter Judd said to Acheson.[17]

Was it not Acheson's duty to protect Foreign Service officers honestly offering dissenting judgments? Acheson would surely have said "yes." He would also have said, probably, that he had carried out this duty by impaneling the various boards that reviewed and re-reviewed the China Hands' records.[18]

To explain why the purge took place, one has to recognize that Acheson could not protect the China Hands all by himself. His own capacity for simply taking people on trust was exhausted by Hiss. In the interest of his president, Acheson could not risk another such episode. Even in the case of Vincent, with whom he had worked so closely, Acheson could take a firm stand only if able to say that Vincent's own co-workers vouched for him. And this he could not do.

Crucial to understanding Acheson's actions is recognition of the fact that the majority of the China Hands did not command confidence within the Foreign Service. They had had a tendency to be clannish. Missionary parentage and mastery of an Oriental language gave many of them a less than egalitarian attitude toward others not similarly blessed. For the most part they identified with one another rather than with "the Service." Before and during the war, they had been visibly at odds with the Japan experts, among them Joseph C. Grew, a patriarch among professional diplomats; and their success against Grew and his allies—in, for example, preventing any formal qualifications of the demand for Japan's unconditional surrender—had been accomplished in alliance with members of the Roosevelt administration whose patriotism many Foreign Service officers doubted.[19] Reflecting possibly typical attitudes, George F. Kennan was to write years later that he and others had felt "very much aware . . . if not of direct Communist penetration, then at least of an unhealthy degree of Communist influence in higher counsels of the Roosevelt administration."[20] At various security or loyalty hearings, Kennan appeared as an expert. He testified to having read Service's reports and to not having found them pro-Communist. He was careful to say, however, that he had no personal knowledge of the man himself.[21]

Skepticism probably prevalent within the Foreign Service is reflected in the diary of John Moors Cabot, an officer from the European service suddenly thrust in 1948 into one of the empty slots in Asia—the post of consulate general in Shanghai—and subsequently brought back to Washington. Concerning John Service, he wrote: "On the one hand, I am revolted at tactics by McCarthy . . . etc.; on the other, Jack S. was undoubtedly guilty of a very serious transgression—more than an indiscretion, and the Department not only took no disciplinary action—it removed essential information from the files we saw on the Selection Board." Concerning Vincent, he wrote, "I did not know enough about Vincent to be absolutely certain that there might not be some evidence that might be unknown to me," and Charles Bohlen of the Russian service cautioned Cabot against getting the Foreign Service Association engaged in Vincent's behalf.[22]

During the McCarthy Era, "guilt by association" became a trite phrase. Sometimes the reality was innocence by association. It protected Alger Hiss when Whittaker Chambers first began retailing his recollections. In Britain it protected Guy Burgess, Donald McLean, "Kim" Philby, and the "fourth man." It was something most of the China Hands lacked. In fact, one may be able to say that those who fell victim suffered from guilt by nonassociation. John Paton Davies was spared during the Acheson era in part because he had been transferred to Moscow and thus became known to members of the more gregarious Russian service. They protected him. Similarly, John Emmerson successfully weathered investigations of 1950 and 1951 because "Japan Hands" such as John M. Allison were prepared to testify to his good character. And Tony Freeman had the best credentials of all. Mike Mansfield vouched for him as a family friend, and Claire Booth Luce attested that he had been invaluable to her in Rome. (She and he made a pact never to discuss China.) Though Freeman never returned to Asia, he suffered no setback in his diplomatic career, ending up as ambassador to Mexico.[23]

Dulles brought himself to defend Bohlen's nomination as ambassador to the Soviet Union, even to cross swords with McCarthy about it, fortified not only by the arid findings of security investigators, but also by testimonials from people who had measured Bohlen's professional caliber, not least Dwight Eisenhower. When Dulles discharged John Paton Davies he heard loud repercussions in his own building. This time John Moors Cabot had no doubts. Many others certified that Davies was a sound Foreign Service officer, and the doyens of the Service—Grew, Norman, Armour, Robert Woods Bliss, William Phillips, and G. Howland Shaw—joined in writing a public letter of protest.[24] Davies' head then was the last to fall.

To argue that Acheson may have had little choice, either politically or morally, is not to deny that wrong was done. It is to suggest that in governments with large, complex personnel systems, the avoidance of wrong depends on a good deal more than the personal character and standards of people at the top. Acheson was prepared to go to considerable lengths not to act unjustly. But he depended on judgments by others. Even when he defended someone, as he did Oliver Clubb, he had to concede that he had not reached the verdict by himself. "I did not study the record," he said to the press, "Because . . . I did not have time to do that."[25] Dulles, by contrast, was disinclined to defend members of the Foreign Service. *His* president had instructed him to get rid of those "who believe in the philosophy of the preceding Administration," and he believed that "a large number fit that description."[26] Left to his own devices, Dulles probably would have gotten rid of many more besides Vincent and Davies, but what he was able to do was severely limited by the nature and processes of the organization over which he presided.

The "primitives" on Capitol Hill dealt with the China Hands shamefully. As was generally true in the period, the press and other media helped by reporting reckless accusations as simply news. Truman, Acheson, and others let themselves respond by creating institutions and processes that, in testing these accusations, let

"loyalty" and "security" acquire loose definitions. Men such as Service and Vincent became branded as something less than patriotic. By anyone's standards, this was wrong, and Acheson said later that the administration's establishment of the Loyalty Review Board had been "a gross mistake and a failure to foresee consequences which were inevitable."[27]

But was Acheson ethically wrong to shift the China Hands away from Asia? Was he ethically wrong to fire Service and to do no more than he did for Ludden or Clubb? Here, it seems to me, the call is much closer, and the ethical choices more acute. The persisting indignation about the China Hands is strongest among people who feel sure the China Hands were right about Chiang. Were it more a matter of pre-World War II "appeasers" or even 1960 "hawks," more intellectuals would probably not be so ardent in condemning reassignments or even the discharge of someone who had broken the rules in order to influence public opinion. Absent belief that the China Hands were right, most people would probably endorse the general principles that Acheson followed, namely, that the executive should respect the express wishes of the public and Congress but should protect careerists who hold dissenting opinions if their fellow careerists certify their professionalism. Are these not good rules and ethical standards for any president or agency head to follow?

Effects of the Purge

Turn now to the proposition that, as a practical matter, the nation paid a high price later for not having the China Hands. Of course one can call Vietnam just the last and deepest in a series of pitfalls. In his book on the China Hands, E. J. Kahn goes so far as to suggest that, had they remained around there might not have been a Korean War.[28] Without that, the whole history of East and South Asia might have been different. Maybe with the expertise of the China Hands, Washington would have stopped talking sooner about the "Sino-Soviet bloc." If so, Vietnam might have been better as an apple of discord between the Communist powers. But the best test of the proposition, probably, is to ask whether expertise such as that of the China Hands might have made a major difference in the mid-1960s, when the Johnson administration decided, in effect, to Americanize the Vietnamese war.

Nearly every American who looks back at those decisions does so with regret. One common line of argument, summarized in the passage from Theodore White, judges American officials to have mistaken a civil war among Vietnamese for an international war between two Vietnamese states; to have overvalued a corrupt neocolonial regime, thus repeating the earlier mistake in China; to have failed to differentiate among varieties of communism; and to have grossly overestimated the capacity of American technology to cope with what was essentially militant peasant nationalism. All this, it is said, the American government and people might have been spared if counseled by experts schooled in the realities of Asia.

This particular argument, however, does not withstand scrutiny. Since the 1960s we have learned a great deal about both American policy-making and conditions in Vietnam. The famous *Pentagon Papers* told part of the Washington story. The Carter administration declassified the bulk of Lyndon Johnson's archives on the subject. Larry Berman's recent *The Planning of a Tragedy* is a good guide to the rich new source material now available. Meanwhile, review of documents released or captured during the war and of retrospective testimony by both South Vietnamese and North Vietnamese officials has produced clearer understanding of conditions in both parts of that country.[29] And the more we learn, the more the people making U.S. policy seem to have been right in their judgments about Vietnam.

In the first place, they seem to have been more right than wrong in regarding the conflict as something other than a civil war. It is true that leaders in Hanoi set "reunification" as an objective. It is also true that they consistently characterized regimes in Saigon as puppets of American imperialism. Scholars who have analyzed North Vietnamese internal politics have concluded that the impetus for active military efforts to achieve reunification came primarily from members of the Politburo with roots in Central or South Vietnam, particularly Le Duan, an Annamese. Until 1964, most of the soldiers and guerrillas fighting against the South Vietnamese government were natives of Central or South Vietnam, though the majority had resided in North Vietnam and had been organized and trained there. And the umbrella National Liberation Front (NLF) was made up of southerners or Annamese, most of whom were not Communists.

The bulk of the evidence now available nevertheless fits a model of international conflict better than a model of internal conflict. In the first half of 1959 there appears to have been intense debate within the Politburo in Hanoi. On one side was Le Duan, who for some period previously had led the clandestine Communist party in South Vietnam. He and his allies argued for committing North Vietnamese resources to bolster the party in the South. As a high-ranking Communist testified later,

> . . . by 1959 the situation in the South had passed into a stage the communists considered the darkest in their lives; almost all their apparatus had been smashed. . . . In the face of this situation the Central Committee saw that it was no longer possible to seize power in the South by means of a peaceful struggle line, since the southern regime, with American assistance, was becoming stronger and not collapsing as had been predicted. Not only had the southern regime not been destroyed, it was instead destroying the Party. Thus it was necessary to have an appropriate line to salvage the situation.[30]

Documents captured by American and South Vietnamese forces tell a similar story. So do histories published in North Vietnam in the 1970s. Opposing Le Duan were members of the Politburo arguing that scarce resources were more needed for development of North Vietnam. But Le Duan won and became general secretary of the Party.

Dispatch to the south of the former southerners trained and armed in the north reversed the decline of Communist fortunes south of the parallel. The second half of 1960 then saw renewed debate in Hanoi. Le Duan again came out the winner. The previous decision had been merely to prevent destruction of the cadres in the south. This time, the party resolved to "liberate" South Vietnam. As one associated tactic, it created the NLF. We now have evidence not only of this decision but of many precautions taken to ensure that the Front would have no control over operating forces, either military or guerrilla. For double safety, reliable Communists were nevertheless to occupy all key posts. That many people in the West saw the NLF otherwise—as authentically southern, not essentially Communist, and the guiding force in opposition to Saigon—was no accident.

Party leaders in Hanoi exerted every effort to make it seem such.
For control of actual fighting forces, these leaders set up a separate
Central Office for South Vietnam (COSVN) staffed with North
Vietnamese officers in a direct chain of command to Hanoi.[31]

Leaders in Hanoi continued to differ among themselves. During
1961 the policies espoused by Le Duan were more or less openly
criticized by, among others, Truong Chinh and General Vo Nguyen
Giap. Although the exact lines of difference are obscure, it seems
that Troung Chinh may have led those who opposed diversion of
resources from development of the north while Giap took the line
that, if liberation was to be pursued, the main instrument should
be the regular army of North Vietnam. Giap may also have been
arguing that Le Duan's policies heightened the risk of drawing the
Americans in and that North Vietnam needed to prepare for a
possible American attack.[32]

At the end of 1963 another round of debate produced a decision
to use regular army units in the south. It is worth noting that this
debate did not take place until December and that it lasted at least
ten days. During the period following the previous decision, the
party in the south again lost ground, this time because of the
success of Saigon's "strategic hamlet" program. By mid–1963 the
"strategic hamlets," however, were losing efficacy. Meanwhile, Bud-
dhists began to demonstrate against the Ngo Dinh Diem regime.
The Americans seemed to be backing away from Diem. Then, in
October, some of South Vietnam's generals assassinated Diem and
his family, and Saigon's whole apparatus of control began to unravel.
It is not clear why, in these circumstances, the North Vietnamese
remained irresolute so long. Nor is it clear why most of 1964 elapsed
before the December 1963 decision began to be put in force and
main-force North Vietnamese regiments showed up in the south. A
later *Hoc Tap* article by Le Duan seems to charge Giap and the
army leadership with excessive cautiousness.[33] During the December
1963 debates several voices warned that the United States might
send in up to 100,000 soldiers; Lieutenant General Nguyen Van Vinh
even said that the total might reach 500,000.[34]

In any case, the decision was made and eventually carried out.
The point is that the terms of debate do not seem those of a civil
war. Even though Le Duan's views might be equated with those of
Cromwell or Lincoln, they could be equally well equated with those

of Hitler regarding Austria, his native ground. The question in each instance was whether or how to use North Vietnam forces that were currently stationed inside North Vietnamese boundaries outside those boundaries.

Rereading appraisals given Lyndon Johnson in 1965, one is struck by the extent to which they describe conditions as, in light of later evidence, they appear actually to have been. Johnson and his advisers believed that, for practical purposes, the army of one Vietnamese nation was invading the territory of another. They judged that the government conducting the invasion expected a comparatively rapid victory if the United States did not intervene. Johnson and his advisers also judged that the invading government planned to take control of all of the other nations. None of these judgments was incorrect.

Similarly, the Johnson administration seems to have had few illusions, if any, about the government of South Vietnam. If Americans in Washington and Saigon made any mistake, it was to underestimate the strength, resiliency, and tenacity of the junta headed by Generals Nguyen Cao Ky and Nguyen Van Thieu. The Military Assistance Command, Vietnam (MACV) and the embassy in Saigon rated the South Vietnamese government low in competence. Washington looked at General Ky, in the words of then Assistant Secretary of State William P. Bundy, as "absolutely bottom of the barrel." Secretary of Defense Robert S. McNamara expressed doubt that Ky would last the year. President Johnson was told that the South Vietnamese army had alarmingly high desertion rates and diminishing battle effectiveness. Secretary of State Dean Rusk believed the guerrillas controlled more than a quarter of the land area of South Vietnam. McNamara thought their area of control even more extensive. All the president's top advisers predicted that, absent strong military action by the United States, the South Vietnamese regime would fall and South Vietnam would be taken over by North Vietnam.[35] Whether this forecast would have proved accurate, we do not know. But it surely cannot serve as evidence of Occidental blindness, for Washington's assessment of the situation almost exactly paralleled Hanoi's.

Third, Johnson and his advisers seem to have been perfectly well aware that the Soviet Union, China, and North Vietnam acted independently rather than as some vast "monolith." They perceived that the Soviets and Chinese competed in supplying aid to North Vietnam, and they recognized that the North Vietnamese probably played one off against the other. They do seem to have been mistaken about the extent to which the North Vietnamese divided into pro-Soviet and pro-Chinese factions and about who belonged to which faction, but their basic diagnosis was on the mark. And memoranda to Johnson in 1965 from State, Defense, and the Central Intelligence Agency (CIA) all spoke coolly of some future moments when Moscow or Peking or both might become channels of communication about terms of settlement.[36]

Fourth, as for gauging the difficulty of fighting the North Vietnamese, the case seems clearest of all. The administration may have underestimated enemy numbers. A review made for President Richard Nixon in 1969 said that the enemy was credited with under 100,000 soldiers in 1965 when the right number should have been around 200,000.[37] Still, Westmoreland said that he would need 175,000 U.S. troops in 1965, another 100,000 in 1966, and more later. After visiting Vietnam in the early autumn of 1965, McNamara predicted a need for a total of 400,000 by the end of 1966 and possibly in excess of 200,000 more in 1967. He also predicted American battle deaths of around a 1,000 a month, and he warned Johnson that there was only a 50 percent chance that the situation would be better in 1967 than in 1965.[38]

The documents presented to Johnson in mid-1965 thus forecast with tolerable accuracy demands for forces and probably for levels of casualties. And, as we now know, Westmoreland's military estimates were just about as on the nose as they possibly could have been. By 1967 maps of South Vietnam had shown areas under government and Communist control in about the same pattern as they had been in 1963. The North Vietnamese had begun to feel serious concern about the position in the south. Their decision for an all-out offensive in early 1968 during the Tet holidays, synchronized with uprisings by hitherto secret cadres in urban areas, seems to have been a deliberate gamble based on fear that the "correlation of forces" would soon become adverse. Speaking of the approaching "*decisive hour,*" the directive for the operation said, "If we do not accomplish our mission, the enemy will link up together, reorganize his strength, consolidate his morale, counterattack us and cause us difficulties and losses."[39] And the initial results for the North Vietnamese were shockingly disappointing. The deputy commander of Communist forces in the Saigon area said later that his side had suffered "enormous, and unanticipated, losses" and that "popular confidence in the Party had been severely damaged."[40] There seems even to have been some consideration in Hanoi of reverting to the pre-1959 strategy of leaving the southerners to their own resources. Truong Chinh said in a broadcast, ". . . at times, under certain circumstances, we must shift to the defensive to gain time, dishearten the enemy, and build up our forces for a new offensive."[41]

But, in fact, the Tet offensive turned the war around the other way. It led directly to Johnson's decision to end the troop buildup, suspend bombing, and open negotiations. It thus started processes that ended several years later in total American withdrawal from Vietnam and, not long afterward, North Vietnamese takeover of the whole country.

Looking back at the deliberations of 1965, it is hard to see what the China Hands or other Asian experts could have said to LBJ that was not in fact said. If his decisions about what to do were incorrect, as most Americans believe, this was not because he was misinformed or misadvised about conditions in Asia.

In retrospect, it seems that what the Johnson administration misjudged was America, not Asia. The President and his advisers knew the war would go on for a long time. Johnson said so in a speech at Johns Hopkins University in the spring of 1965. He had been told that casualties would run at or above rates of the Korean War, and he and everyone around him were old enough to remember how public opinion had soured against that war. Yet the majority of documents circulating in the executive branch expressed confidence that Congress and the people would back administration policy, come what may. Recommending that Westmoreland get the troops he had requested, McNamara wrote: "Even though casualties will increase and the war will continue for some time, the United States public will support this course of action because it is a combined military-political program designed and likely to bring about a favorable solution to the Vietnam problem."[42] In one memorandum McGeorge Bundy suggested diffidently some inspection of what "a really full political and public relations campaign" might entail. The suggestion was never followed up. Aside from Vice President Hubert Humphrey, who reminded Johnson of what the Korean War had done to Truman's domestic programs and personal popularity, no one explored the possibility that the McNamara assumption might prove wrong. And LBJ himself evidenced less concern about possible doubters than about "hawks" who might criticize him for not giving Westmoreland all that he asked.[43]

Why was this so? Why were these Americans more or less right about Asia but blind to what might happen in America? And to swing back to the China Hands, how does one account for the government's not being equally dim-sighted regarding Asia?

To answer either question fully would take many pages, most of them simply posing additional questions. Framing sketchy answers and taking the second question first, one has to note that the purge of the China Hands did not, in fact, deprive the government of all expertise about Asia. The State Department kept in service in Asia Everett Drumwright and a few others who had not been hostile to Chiang. Moreover, it retained throughout the services of a skilled group of experts on Japan. All good members of the club, they survived the danger of a wartime purge and went on after the war to dominate the Asian Bureau.

Meanwhile, other parts of the government also nourished Asian expertise. The army and navy had had intelligence officers trained in Asian languages. A few were purged along with the China Hands. The majority, however, had good connections with the Nationalists or the patronage of someone such as General Douglas MacArthur or General Albert Wedemeyer or Admiral Charles O. Cooke; and they remained on duty, training successors. The new Central Intelligence Agency provided a hiding place for other Asian experts, including some who lacked Nationalist blessing. With the Korean conflict it became a magnet for well-bred, well-educated young men wanting service on the front line of the Cold War. It was the club of clubs—an official Skull and Bones. And it had the further advantage of directors, first General Walter Bedell Smith and then Allen Dulles, whose attitudes were more Acheson's than John Foster Dulles's. When McCarthy wanted to make a run at William Bundy, then at CIA, Allen Dulles resisted. Bundy said later, "there was an element of tribal loyalty in the way Allen handled this . . . —a feeling for the comradeship of the CIA but also a tribal feeling toward a set of people who were in law firms, entered government when the need was felt, and could be invited back to the house."[44]

All through the 1950s, CIA built up its foreign stations and its domestic analytical offices. As Southeast Asia became a more and more prominent theater of the Cold War, more and more of the agency's bright lights went, or turned their attention, to that part of the world. The same held for service intelligence arms. By the mid-1960s, MACV had extraordinary resources for gathering information, and Washington had plenty of analysts with enough knowledge and background to make sense of the data sent back.

The documents now available show a good deal of debate among these analysts. The State Department's Bureau of Intelligence and Research and CIA's Office of National Estimates generally took a darker view than did MACV or the armed services or other parts of CIA of the prospects for the Saigon regime.[45] Sometimes sharp words were exchanged. All this suggests that close-knit clubs permitted a capacity for dissent to survive within the government despite the earlier purge.

To say this, and to stop there, would be, however, to ignore the real point behind what White and others have said. The distinctive characteristic of the China Hands who were purged was not their knowledge of China. It was their openness to the notion that a Communist government for China might not be bad. That was what was purged. And that was what remained purged. The State and CIA analysts pessimistic about Saigon were saying regretfully that they thought the United States would lose. But no one inside the government, so far as one can now tell, was even considering accommodating North Vietnam on North Vietnamese terms.

Should there have been people in the government arguing for such policies? Should the bureaucracy have kept people at work during World War II developing cases for accommodation with the Axis states? Should it now have people paid for advocating dissolution of NATO? Should it have kept on duty China Hands who were opponents of the alliance with Chiang? Are these proper functions for careerists, or are they instead functions to be performed somewhere else in the political marketplace?

And how do these questions dovetail with those raised by evidence of the Johnson administration's failure to understand American aspects of its Vietnam policy (since the positions not explored within the bureaucracy were precisely those around which opposition to the war would cluster)? Would people in the government have appreciated the domestic risks of their decisions more if the later public argument had been better prefigured in its own internal debates? Looking back at intragovernmental debate on Vietnam and the subsequent public debate, one is struck by the extent to which differences were, at the heart of it, differences in moral judgments.

As members of the Kennedy administration before them, members of the Johnson administration talked about protecting interests, preventing the fall of dominoes, and so on. With McNamara in the lead, they tried to make success or failure something measurable in hard numbers, including "body counts." But almost no one showed evidence of really believing South Vietnam itself to be important. Under all the hard language lay basic concern about the image and reality of American behavior and loyalty toward "a friend." In that sense, it was a highly ethical question. Rusk captured the essential position of practically everyone in the administration when he wrote Johnson in mid-1965, "So long as the South Vietnamese are prepared to fight for themselves, we cannot abandon them. . . ."[46]

But there were at least two alternative positions representing different moral priorities. One figured in Hubert Humphrey's counsel, when he said, in effect, that the highest good consisted in getting on with business at home. The majority of the public came to have something close to this view, mirrored dovishly or hawkishly in various preferences, all of which had the effect of getting the war ended. A second position was that of people who appropriated to themselves the adjective "antiwar." They subscribed to the view that the United States supported the wrong side in Vietnam and compounded evil by killing good Vietnamese on behalf of bad ones.

As a practical matter, it would not have been hard to foresee growing popularity for different definitions of the moral issues than those prevalent in official circles when the critical decisions were made. Something of the sort had happened during most wars in American history. It was not unknown in Britain and in other countries. Possibly, just possibly, debates in Washington in 1965 might have had as much realism regarding America as regarding Asia if the decision-making processes required looking at alternative ways of framing the moral issues and looking ahead to see whether today's right and wrong would seem the same tomorrow. And indeed, principles and arrangements that protect independence of judgment within the government probably promote that objective as well as more workaday ones.

Ethics and Diplomacy

What, then, can we make of these two historical cases that were touched, either directly or indirectly, by the China Hands? For the subject of the relationship between ethics and diplomacy, what are the implications of the China Hands' legacy?

I believe first that the cases argue that even though one can have instances in which the choices overlap completely, as in the China Hands' decision of whether to tell the truth or not, they are rare. Ordinarily in the dilemmas that present themselves to decision makers, the ethical questions are inseparable, but they are different and they have to be thought that way.

One has to recognize that diplomatic questions are not ethical questions. The fundamental mistake that the Johnson administration made in 1965 regarding Vietnam was to assume that the diplomatic question was an ethical question, to be decided on those terms and on those grounds. But neither is the reverse true. Ethical questions are not diplomatic questions. This, it seems to me, explains at least some of the difference between Acheson and Dulles. Acheson, as we have seen, clearly appears as someone who was genuinely sensitive to ethical issues. Dulles, by contrast, at least in those decisions that he made like dismissing John Carter Vincent, firing John Paton Davies, and employing Scott McLeod and endorsing what he was doing in the Department of State, demonstrates a striking callousness. One senses that what mattered to Dulles with the China Hands were the practical results and that ethical questions of whether the decisions were morally right or wrong were not important. In this regard, he appears as the reverse of the problem.

What we have to recognize is that ethical issues have inescapable practical dimensions. To ignore this is to risk great peril. Moreover, we also have to acknowledge that practical issues have inescapable ethical dimensions. The task, of course, is to see both of them, to see them in the round, and to see them in all of their dimensions.

Consider, for a moment, the term, "political expediency." In a way, that is what Hubert Humphrey and Clark Clifford were arguing to Lyndon Johnson. They did not say that the moral course of action was to abandon the South Vietnamese. Instead, they argued for political expediency, saying that there were "other considerations" such as domestic programs, the future of the party, and the general welfare that suggested another course of action than the one being followed in Vietnam. I believe that deciding where the line falls between political expediency and political responsibility is the hardest issue for decision-makers to resolve. It lies at the very center of ethical issues for people in positions of responsibility.

How do any of us resolve this problem or learn how and where to draw that line? I do not believe that there are any sets of precepts or that there is any way that we can look up the answers in the back of a book. The only way to develop one's abilities and sensitivities in this regard is to look at cases like the China Hands and to think about how the ethical and practical dimensions of problems were confronted by those who actually had to make the decisions.

I do think, however, Acton gave bad advice. Historians are poorly equipped to sit as hanging judges. We do better when we try instead to make people of the past comprehensible in the present. But when those people themselves regretted what occurred—as Acheson did the Loyalty-Security proceedings and Johnson and his circle Vietnam—then historians may perhaps be licensed to say how they think the particular pitfall might have been avoided. Exercising that license, I close with the sobering observation that what might have been of most use to Truman and Acheson and to LBJ would have been some standard process for paying serious attention to moral and ethical dimensions of issues treated instead as legal or administrative or diplomatic or military. Thinking about how to do this ought to rank high on the agenda of anyone seeking to remember the China Hands and to undertake any project commemorating Mike Mansfield.

Notes

1. Theodore H. White *In Search of History: A Personal Adventure* (New York: Harper and Row, 1978), p. 395.

2. Quoted in Dean G. Acheson, *Present at the Creation: My Years in the State Department* (New York: W. W. Norton, 1969), p. 361. Information has recently come to light showing that Acheson, along with other

Covington and Burling partners, advised Hiss when the House Un-American Activities Committee was interrogating him and that, if Acheson had not been appointed secretary of state, he might have been one of Hiss's lawyers. If publicized at this time, these facts could have caused problems for Acheson, and a thorough cynic could argue—wrongly, I think—that Acheson spoke as he did in order to keep Hiss quiet. See Allen Weinstein, *Perjury: The Hiss-Chambers Case* (New York: Alfred A. Knopf, 1978), pp. 10, 17, 181, 194, 384–386.

3. E. J. Kahn, Jr., *The China Hands: America's Foreign Service Officers and What Befell Them* (New York: Viking, 1965), originally serialized in *The New Yorker*, is a clear, informative account, sympathetic to the China Hands. Gary May, *China Scapegoat: The Diplomatic Ordeal of John Carter Vincent* (Washington: New Republic Books, 1979) is a scholarly work on a single China Hand. Earl Latham, *The Communist Controversy in Washington: From the New Deal to McCarthy* (Cambridge: Harvard University Press, 1966) is one scholar's only partially successful effort to review evidence of the period on the supposition that there might have been fire behind the smoke. Chapters 8–10 deal with the China Hands.

4. John S. Service, *The AMERASIA Papers: Some Problems in the History of US-China Relations* (Berkeley: University of California Press, 1971) gives Service's perspective, together with documents.

5. Russell Buhite, *Patrick J. Hurley and American Foreign Policy* (Ithaca: Cornell University Press, 1973) is the fullest study of Hurley likely ever to be written.

6. Kahn, *The China Hands*, pp. 237–239.

7. Ibid., pp. 10, 17, 230, 246.

8. Ibid., pp. 242–243. O. Edmund Clubb, *The Witness and I* (New York: Columbia University Press, 1975) has the details of his ordeals on the Hill.

9. May, *China Scapegoat.*

10. Ibid., p. 165.

11. Kahn, *The China Hands*, p. 255.

12. Ibid., 257 ff.

13. May, *China Scapegoat*, p. 186.

14. Acheson, *Present at the Creation*, pp. 360–361.

15. Thomas C. Reeves, *The Life and Times of Joe McCarthy* (New York: Stein and Day, 1982) gives a full picture, including evidence on how J. Edgar Hoover supplied covert staff work for McCarthy.

16. Ample evidence of the constant pressure on the administration appears in the now declassified records of executive sessions in the *Historical Series* publications of the Senate Foreign Relations Committee.

17. May, *China Scapegoat*, pp. 166, 208.

18. Acheson denounced Dulles for having Davies's case reviewed by a board unqualified to appraise professional competence. Dean G. Acheson, *Private Thoughts on Public Affairs* (New York: Harper and Row, 1967), pp. 168–170.

19. See Waldo H. Heinrichs, Jr., *American Ambassador: Joseph C. Grew and the Development of the American Diplomatic Tradition* (Boston: Little, Brown, 1966), pp. 372 ff.

20. George F. Kennan, *Memoirs, 1950–1963* (Boston: Little, Brown, 1972), p. 191.

21. Kahn, *The China Hands*, pp. 221–222.

22. J. M. Cabot, *First Line of Defense: Fifty Years' Experiences of a Career Diplomat* (Washington, D.C.: Georgetown School of the Foreign Service, n.d.), pp. 80–83.

23. Kennan did defend Davies as someone known to him: Kennan, *Memoirs*, p. 200 ff. John K. Emmerson, *The Japanese Thread, A Life in the Foreign Service* (New York: Holt, Rinehart, and Winston, 1978), pp. 307–342; and John M. Allison, *Ambassador from the Prairie; or Allison Wonderland* (Boston: Houghton Mifflin, 1973), p. 115, tell Emmerson's story. On Freeman, see Kahn, *The China Hands*, pp. 18 ff.

24. Cabot, *First Line of Defense*, pp. 96–100; Kahn, *The China Hands*, p. 34.

25. *Time*, LIX (March 17, 1952), p. 18.

26. Stephen E. Ambrose, *Eisenhower the President* (New York: Simon and Schuster, 1984), pp. 64–65.

27. Acheson, *Private Thoughts*, p. 166.

28. Kahn, *The China Hands*, p. 6.

29. Larry Berman, *Planning a Tragedy: The Americanization of the War in Vietnam* (New York: W. W. Norton, 1982). Among the more important assemblages of Vietnamese material accessible to people who (like myself) do not read Vietnamese are *Vietnam Documents and Research Notes*, a series of translations issued from the 1960s until the mid-1970s by the Joint United States Public Affairs Office in Saigon; U.S. Department of State, "Working Papers on North Viet-Nam's Role in the War in South Viet-Nam" (1968), the appendices of which consist of North Vietnamese publications and captured North Vietnamese and Viet Cong documents; Patrick J. McGarvey, *Visions of Victory: Selected Vietnamese Communist Military Writings, 1964–1968* (Stanford: The Hoover Institution, 1969); and Gareth Porter (ed.), *Vietnam: The Definitive Documentation of Human Decisions*, 2 vols. in progress (Stanfordville, N.Y.: Coleman, 1979). Of particular interest are the so-called CRIMP documents, the notebooks of a high-level Communist leader captured in 1966 in "Operation CRIMP"

and published as Appendix Item 301 in the "Working Paper," *Outline History of the Vietnam Workers' Party* (Hanoi: Foreign Languages Press, 1972); and Ta Xuan Linh, "How Armed Struggle Began in South Vietnam": *Vietnam Courier,* No. 22 (March 1974).

30. The quotation is from Jeffrey Race, *War Comes to Long An: Revolutionary Conflict in a Vietnamese Province* (Berkeley: University of California Press, 1972), pp. 109–110. Race argues that a Communist victory was practically inevitable because the Communists were much closer to peasants and villagers while non-Communist regimes were hopelessly linked with exploitative landlords. But he bases his book on a large quantity of authentic documentary evidence (some of it available on film from the University of Chicago as "Vietnamese Materials Collected by Jeffrey Race"), and he constructs his case without the myth-making characteristic of most comparable literature. Further evidence on the 1959 debates appears in Carlyle A. Thayer, "The Origins of the National Front for the Liberation of South Viet-Nam" (Ph.D. dissertation: Australian National University, 1977); and, more summarily, in King C. Chen, "Hanoi's Three Decisions and the Escalation of the Vietnam War," *Political Science Quarterly,* XC (July 1975), pp. 245–248; and, in more detail, in William J. Duiker, *The Communist Road to Power in Vietnam* (Boulder: Westview Press, 1981), pp. 177–190.

31. Race, *War Comes to Long An,* pp. 121–122; Thayer, "The Origins of the National Front," *passim*; Chen, "Hanoi's Three Decisions," pp. 248–251; and Duiker, *The Communist Road to Power,* pp. 197–199. Documents on North Vietnamese arrangements for the NLF and COSVN are conveniently available.

32. Wallace J. Thies, *When Governments Collide: Coercion and Diplomacy in the Vietnam Conflict, 1964–1968* (Berkeley: University of California Press, 1980), pp. 242–244; and Duiker, *The Communist Road to Power,* pp. 205–212, summarize the debates among North Vietnamese. Douglas Pike, *History of Vietnamese Communism, 1925–1976* (Stanford: The Hoover Institution, 1978), pp. 116–118, suggests this interpretation of Giap's writings. Another significant collection of documents, also available on film from the University of Chicago is "Documents on the National Liberation Front and the People's Revolutionary Party gathered by Douglas Pike . . . "

33. Thies, *When Governments Collide,* p. 261.

34. Ibid., pp. 249 ff. and 330–331; and Chen, "Hanoi's Three Decisions," pp. 252 ff.

35. George C. Herring, *America's Longest War: The United States and Vietnam 1950–1975* (New York: John Wiley, 1979), p. 138 (quoting William P. Bundy, then assistant secretary of state for East Asia); and McNamara

memorandum of 20 July 1965 in *The Pentagon Papers: The Defense Department History of United States Decision-Making on Vietnam*, the Senator Gravel Edition, III, 4 vols. (Boston: The Beacon Press, n.d.), p. 620. See Berman, *Planning a Tragedy, passim*.

36. Thies, *When Governments Collide*; Allan E. Goodman, *The Lost Peace: America's Search for a Negotiated Settlement of the Vietnam War* (Stanford: The Hoover Institution, 1978); and Gareth Porter, *A Peace Denied* (Bloomington, Ind.: University of Indiana Press, 1975) detail the various negotiation efforts. Janos Radvanyi, *Delusion and Reality: Gambits, Hoaxes, and Diplomatic One-Upmanship in Vietnam* (South Bend, Ind.: Gateway, 1978), details some of the exchanges in East European channels.

37. Thies, *When Governments Collide*, p. 415, citing the Nixon administration's review of Vietnam policy, Nation Security Study Memorandum 1, the test of which is in 92 Cong., 2 sess., *Congressional Record* (10–11 May 1972), pp. E4975 ff. and E5008 ff. *The Pentagon Papers*, Gravel Edition, III, 441, cites 1965 MACV estimates crediting the enemy with 137,000 to 153,000 men. The difficulty of interpreting order of battle estimates is fully documented in transcripts of the 1984 lawsuit brought by General Westmoreland against CBS.

38. Westmoreland to the Joint Chiefs of Staff, 14 June 1965, "The War in Vietnam: Classified Histories by the National Security Council: Development of Major U.S. Forces to Vietnam: July 1965" (University Press of America microfilm); McNamara to the president, 30 November 1965, *The Pentagon Papers*, Gravel Edition, IV, p. 622.

39. "Two Directives for Tet," *Vietnam Documents and Research Notes*, no. 29 (April 1968).

40. Race, *War Comes to Long An*, pp. 269–271.

41. Quoted in Thies, *When Governments Collide*, pp. 345–346.

42. McNamara to the president, 1 July 1965, "The War in Vietnam: Classified Histories."

43. McGeorge Bundy to the president, 1 July 1965, "The War in Vietnam: Classified Histories"; Humphrey to the president, 15 February 1965, Hubert H. Humphrey, *Education of a Public Man: My Life and Politics* (Garden City, N.Y.: Doubleday, 1976), pp. 318–324. Thies, *When Governments Collide*, pp. 184–185, makes the point that in August 1967 Johnson killed a possibly promising negotiation opportunity because he chose to step up the air war against North Vietnam in order to undercut Senate Armed Services Committee hearings expected to push the thesis that the administration was not fighting hard enough.

44. Leonard Mosley, *Dulles: A Biography of Eleanor, Allen and John Foster Dulles and Their Family Network* (New York: Dial, 1978), p. 323. Cord Meyer, *Facing Reality: From World Federalism to the CIA* (New

York: Harper and Row, 1980), Chapter 4, provides further evidence on the CIA's protection of its own.

45. On differences within the intelligence community see Robert L. Gallucci, *Neither Peace nor Honor: The Politics of American Military Policy in Viet-Nam* (Baltimore: Johns Hopkins University Press, 1976), pp. 64–71; and 94 Cong., 1 sess., House Select Committee on Intelligence Activities, *Hearings on the Performance of the Intelligence Community.*

46. Rusk to the president, 1 July 1965, "The War in Vietnam: Classified Histories."

JOHN F. MELBY

6

The China Hands and McCarthyism: An Overview

Not long after Senator Joseph McCarthy died, Peggy Durdin, the very perceptive wife of the *New York Times* correspondent in China, said to me that the real tragedy of the McCarthy phenomenon was not really the destruction of the American Foreign Service group, dreadful as that was. The real tragedy was that whole generations of young Americans were being successfully conditioned to believe that anything was justified in the name of national security. If Peggy had had sufficient extended vision, she could have added that by 1960 this conditioning would make Watergate a virtual certainty.

Once I had thought—or hoped—that the American rebellion against Vietnam coming on the heels of the debacle in China would do two things: first, initiate a long-needed examination of the roots of American foreign policy; second, produce something useful out of the student upheavals of the late 1960s. Neither of these occurred. In Europe as in America, they were simply destructive, offering nothing to replace what had been destroyed. It was a wasted effort.

Today we have an administration—and I have to lay some blame on all three branches of government—that is rather quietly proceeding with the militarization of American society, together with too many of the restrictive measures that go along with this kind of change. It is getting away with it, and it is doing so in the name of national security—whatever that means.

For this reason, I think it is worthwhile for a moment to examine some of the roots of McCarthyism. The movement to which his name has become attached, probably unfairly is called that only because he was such an erratically flamboyant character. In the Senate, for example, McCarran, Hickenlooper, Jenner, and Eastland were active long before McCarthy even mentioned communism. The Senate Internal Security Subcommittee was still busy when he was long gone. But the roots are much deeper than that. Eric Goldman made a best-selling reputation with his book, *Rendezvous with Destiny*.[1] His thesis was that people from all lands and all cultures have come here to the melting pot and that out of this process came the American man and woman. True enough, as far as it went. But it was Edward Digby Baltzell, a Philadelphia mainline sociologist, who went farther back with his *The Protestant Establishment: Aristocracy and Caste in America*.[2] His contention was that the colonial aristocracy in America was WASP—white, Anglo-Saxon, Protestant—and that it took control of American society and has kept that control ever since. Later on, as waves of non-WASP immigrants started pouring in, making the WASP a decided minority in the process, the aristocrat had the wit to co-opt the brightest boys and girls of the immigrant groups into aristocratic society, thereby providing bridges to the immigrant and getting across the message that immigrants would be accepted as soon as they had jobs, learned English, and adopted WASP values. Without this, the aristocrat would become caste and replaceable—as has happened so often before in other societies. People who held these values were conservative, highly individualistic in giving primacy to the individual as opposed to the individual's contribution to society, wary of encroachment by the state, suspicious of alien—meaning mostly European—immigrant concepts of the role of the state, and woefully ignorant of how the world looks through the eyes of others.

This was a set of values that the mass of immigrants in the contemporary circumstances of America had little difficulty in accepting and translating into more freedom and opportunity for more people than most had ever dreamed possible anywhere else. If it was not exactly the golden mountain in the dreams of indentured Chinese railroad coolies or the free lunch of Jews from eastern European ghettoes, still it was not something that the majority of immigrants were about to turn their backs on. Hostility to Marxism— to be known as communism—when added to Soviet military power could easily be simplified into a mortal threat to every value that we Americans have ever professed. To this cauldron I should add the Soviet use of a kind of Eurasian subversion and espionage, that at least until World War II was unknown to Americans and for which we happily still show little aptitude, let alone finesse. My use of the word simplify may be misleading, because there is no longer anything simple in the nuclear age, even if President Reagan could casually drop some remark about Armageddon in our time to a horrified Israeli ambassador.[3] As understandable, even as natural, as a basic conflict between our two systems undoubtedly is, the only simple thing about it is that Armageddon is a totally unacceptable solution. I cannot conceive that even Senator McCarthy could have taken it seriously.

McCarthy's attack was by no means just on the Department of State and its China Hands, even though they were the ones who suffered the most publicly. The attack was largely on those identified as WASP establishment. The attackers tended to come from groups that at one time or another had been discriminated against and remembered it—Catholics, Irish, Jews, Italians, southerners, Protestant fundamentalists. I should say here that I am not in any way referring to cases of genuine espionage, such as the Canadian spy case of 1946, Klaus Fuchs, the Rosenbergs, and Judith Coplon, all involved in nuclear espionage, virtually all of eastern European origin, fairly new arrivals, and of very dubious loyalty.

The range of victims was broad, from John Carter Vincent, career minister and former head of the State Department office of Far Eastern Affairs, to Owen Lattimore, a former editor for the Institute of Pacific Affairs and a White House adviser, to the secretary of the Air Force, to an Annie Moss who worked on a steam table in a Pentagon cafeteria and quite clearly never had a clue as to what the uproar was all about. It has been estimated that some 11,500 people were directly involved in personal and public attack, litigation, and loss of careers and jobs.[4] Virtually none of these cases were handled by the usual legal channels. All were handled administratively, a new and uncharted method for lawyers. This was something that we had never known before in the United States, but in which we have since acquired a great deal of expertise. There is no way of estimating the damage done to the country at large by intimidation or effective silencing of large numbers of people on topics about which any democracy needs free and open discussion. I am not suggesting that the McCarthy period was unique. There were the Salem witch trials, after all; the infamous Alien and Sedition Acts of 1801; and the Mitchell Palmer raids of 1919. The uniqueness of McCarthyism was its pervasiveness, and that emerged as a by-product of instant communications around the world.

It is safe to say, however, that this modern witch-hunt launched by McCarthy in the name of national security began with an attack upon the Foreign Service. In early February 1950, the senator was speaking at a rally in Wheeling, West Virgina. He claimed to be holding in his hand a list of 205 people known to Secretary of State Dean Acheson to be Communists yet still under the employ of the department. When pressed by the department and members of the Senate Foreign Relations Committee, McCarthy proved unable to substantiate his claim. Senator Millard Tydings, who chaired a special subcommittee to investigate these charges against the State Department personnel, felt compelled to call them "a hoax and a fraud . . . an effort to inflame the American people with a wave of hysteria and fear on an unbelievable scale." Tydings reported that McCarthy's allegations constituted "the most nefarious campaign of half-truths and untruths in the history of this republic" and then expressed confidence in the public servants who ran the department and served in the Foreign Service.[5] This should have deflated McCarthy and his efforts, but it did not. He simply continued. For most of those whose names now had been publicized, the future was to be dark.

For those in the Foreign Service, and particularly the China Hands or China language people, the pervasiveness of McCarthyism would cause them to suffer in many ways for a variety of reasons and perceived associations. I would like to insert a personal note at this point. Although I was stationed in China for a period of years, I was never a Chinese language officer. I was sent to Chungking originally because of my Moscow background to follow the activities of the Soviet embassy. The Russian ambassador and several of his staff turned out to be friends from Moscow. The embassy was behaving with scrupulous diplomatic propriety for reasons of Soviet self-interest rather than any niceties of principle. After a few months, China, as it does with most people, began to get under my skin and I have been at it ever since. China, as far as I know, never had anything to do with my problems with security and never figured in my security hearings. My guilt, if you wish to call it that, was a close association that still goes on with a very well-known American literary lady who still is not quite sure where China is located but of whose political activities the authorities in the 1950s took a very dim view.

The baffling point is that the views and the reporting of those of us who served in China after the surrender of Japan in 1945 were never really challenged, although they differed in no important respect from those who had been there before us. There was not even any toning down of what we reported, if for no better reason than that the civil war that broke out in the fall of 1945 cut us all off so completely that we really knew nothing of what was happening politically or domestically in the United States or, for that matter, anyplace else in the world. So for me, the years from 1945 to 1949, apart from China, really do not exist. What did happen is that as we closed shop in China we were assigned to posts other than China and soon altogether out of Asia. In some cases some of us were penalized much more harshly. I can, therefore, personally describe the full impact of McCarthyism, without being at all defensive about what I wrote from China, beyond knowing that no one in a position to do anything was paying the slightest attention in Washington. The attacks were for the most part on those who had been in China during the stewardship of General Joseph Stilwell and the ambassadorship of that very proper model of a modern major general, Patrick J. Hurley. What we can now document, but have long suspected, is that the China Lobby, both American and Chinese members, had assiduously been laying the foundations to destroy selectively those who questioned the right to wear the "Mandate of Heaven" that Chiang Kai-shek had assumed and exercised so arrogantly.[6]

The attack on the China Hands was also largely a coincidence of timing. The Democrats had won five elections in a row, the last one without the extraordinary leadership of Franklin Roosevelt. The Republicans feared that another loss would kill the party. China, with which many Americans had come to feel a special relationship, was suddenly slipping into the communist orbit. How could China do this to us after all we had done for it? The State Department was a very small organization (the total officer corps was only 721 when I entered in 1937), and its people almost automatically by virtue of their profession had either largely given up or lost ties and roots to any particular locale and hence had no domestic supporters. The Foreign Service, and especially the China group, was a natural target. By the time the fury had abated, there was no one left in the department still working on Asia whose expertise on China antedated 1949. Abroad, Foreign Service officers in general either stopped reporting what they were learning or tailored their reports to fit what they thought Washington wanted to hear. Through the 1950s merely to have been in the State Department was enough to make most people cross over to the other side of the street.

It is difficult, of course, for many to conceive of what life was really like in those days. Here, the case of the return of General Douglas MacArthur to the United States in 1951 is particularly instructive. It is extraordinary how rapidly that incredible event has faded from the public memory, but anyone stationed in Washington at the time remembers it acutely. MacArthur was relieved of his command by President Harry Truman on the grounds that he had exceeded his authority and usurped the functions of civilians and their control of the military. Truman, it must be stated, had handled the Korean War in a rather confused fashion, changing objectives back and forth, so that the American people did not know what the real objectives were. But this was no excuse for the way that MacArthur had behaved. So in the end, Truman felt compelled to relieve him from all command in the Far East and to retire him permanently from active duty.

MacArthur returned to the United States, however, to what was billed as a "hero's welcome." The rhetoric that was spread around Washington at that time, particularly in Congress, was something that one had to experience to believe. I think that the welcome he received in New York was probably genuine, and it may well have been elsewhere—but not everywhere. It just so happened that I was scheduled weeks in advance to deliver a speech before the Milwaukee Council on Foreign Relations on the subject of China the very day of MacArthur's visit to that city. After my address, I retired to a pub located across from City Hall overlooking the central square where I could sit down and watch his arrival and reception by what had been described as "a million people." I thus had the advantage of watching the scene on television in the pub and then looking out the window and seeing what was actually happening in the square outside. Television viewers watched as the cameras panned back and forth over the same crowd to give the appearance of a massive throng of supporters. But in looking out of the window, I could see that there was a crowd of not more than 5,000. This was the so-called million from Milwaukee. One therefore has to wonder how much television coverage faked the other appearances as well. This fakery and the general hysteria that accompanied MacArthur's return was symptomatic of McCarthyism and its perverse influence upon America.

All during those years, the American media reported about China only the official line of Secretary of State John Foster Dulles and Assistant Secretary of State for Far Eastern Affairs Walter Robertson.[7] This made thin reading. Before World War II, Cartier-Bresson, the famous photographer, had published an international best-seller, with a gorgeous volume on the art treasures of Russia. He did another one on China after the war. No one would publish it. He finally brought it out at his own expense, despite advice not to do so. It sold exactly five copies in the United States. This was typical of what was being published about China during those years and of the refusal by the American public to acknowledge information of any kind about the Chinese during this period.

There is a fashionable line of lament over what happened to the China Hands like Davies and Service that ends: "If only we had listened to them, the twenty-year freeze in relations with China would never have happened. The Korean war could have been avoided. The disaster of Vietnam would not have occurred." Taken as a literal statement, this is probably correct. The reporting was impeccably accurate, the recommendations eminently sensible. But it is fatuous now to argue that the reporting and the recommendations would or could have been welcomed in Washington at that time. This is a Carlylian theory of history, or a devil theory if you prefer, that great men or just men affect the course of history. I disagree with this. You cannot move one or even several pieces of the mosaic without changing the whole pattern. There are currents in history that men may shape, alter, or bend, but never reverse.

There is a curiously Pollyannaish tone in the old cliché about an idea whose time has come. The harsh reality of life is that the right times for ideas are few and far between. Shakespeare put it well:

There is a tide in the affairs of men,
Which, taken at the flood, leads on to fortune;
Omitted, all the voyage of their life
Is bound in shallows and in miseries.

It is doubtless fortunate that few of us are gifted, or cursed, with accurate foresight. The temptation to do nothing might well be irresistible; coincidentally, it could well reinforce a self-fulfilling prophecy of doom and failure.

The China Hands, right as they were, reported what the American public for the most part did not want to hear and did not believe for all the reasons that I have at least implied so far. It was a tragedy for which the China officers paid dearly. More to the point, it was a tragedy for which the American people are still paying an infinitely greater price long after most people have forgotten there ever were China Hands who happened to see China's future with remarkable clarity. Part of the myopia stems from what Barbara Tuchman in her book, *The March of Folly*, calls woodenheadedness, an urge by policy-makers who should know better to pursue self-deflating policies, even when feasible alternatives are openly advocated by knowledgeable critics.[8] And part of the myopia comes from popular, meaning mostly the youths', disenchantment with the study of history. The apathy seems to reflect the colloquial eloquence of Henry Ford who once announced to a waiting world, "History is bunk."

It is possible, of course, that Henry Ford was right, but the circumstances that produced the misguided public attitudes that nullified any wisdom the China Hands may have expressed are still very much with us and show few signs of changing. The question, then and today, has to be whether as a people we or our leaders have acquired the additional knowledge and understanding of the challenge that undoubtedly confronts us and that must be answered or accommodated one way or another. Sadly, I am afraid, the answer has to be no. And just as sadly I would add that I think former Senator George McGovern, who received an enthusiastic round of applause in the debate in Atlanta, was right when he said, "In the name of fighting communism, we have embraced nearly every scoundrel around the world."[9]

I said earlier I had hoped one result of the Vietnam debacle would be a national reexamination of the roots of American foreign policy. There has been a tendency among many Americans to assume that foreign policy began with the end of World War II when world leadership was forced on us at a time when we would really have preferred to avoid that awesome responsibility. There is evidence this is still true, if for no better reason than that Americans have a compulsion to be loved, and no one loves the rich boy on the block. The fact is that the tenets of U.S. foreign policy have deep roots, most of them in colonial times, that have influenced our behavior for so long they are simply taken for granted.

One of the more influential of these root causes is a Biblical one. The Puritans had a sense of mission. The new Americans were a Chosen People with a destiny and a new purpose in this world. It was no accident that the settlers in Massachusetts spoke of a shining city on a hill, a new Zion. Bishop Berkeley caught the mood in the eighteenth century when he rimed about "westward the tide of empire flows. . . ." His empire did not stop at the Golden Gate, but jumped the Pacific to China, which would become the essence and symbol of the missionary movement. WASP self-righteousness was fundamental to the value system that the immigrant was expected to adopt, and he found little difficulty in doing so. In effect, he became more Catholic than the Pope. The underlying assumption was that anything is possible for the true believer; its military expression was the doctrine of General U. S. Grant that held that if you simply apply enough power, anything can be accomplished. It was a gory doctrine to which every army in the world soon aspired, until the discovery of the atomic bomb forever changed everything anyone had ever thought about war. Hence, I had hoped for a new and conscious evaluation and judgment on the validity of the assumptions. It is, of course, altogether possible that out of such an evaluation we might have decided the Pilgrims were quite right in exterminating the Pequot Indians, but at least it would have been a conscious judgment reached in contemporary conditions.

This book asks several sets of questions. The first set deals with the influence of domestic politics and perceptions upon American relations with Asia and is the easiest to answer. U.S. policy toward Asia is still influenced, as it always has been, by gross misinterpretations and outright, if not always deliberate, fabrications. One needs only a general knowledge of the sordid history of the Kuo-mintang, the origins and rise to power of Chiang Kai-shek, and the incredible machinations of the Soong clan to realize how completely the American public and much of its government were gulled for literally decades into adulatory support of an appalling regime. The American anti-Communist paranoia has encouraged either active support or at least tolerance of any alternative to the alleged source of all that is evil in this world.

Since its inception a century and a half ago, the American missionary movement may well have been the single most important element in influencing foreign policy toward China. Coming from a society in which the church, regardless of the constitutional ban to the contrary, has always been the unofficial setter of community morals and standards, missionaries have never been shy about informing Washington and the public of their interests. The Puritan ethic alliance of God and Mammon worked as well in China as it did elsewhere.

Another set of questions concerns the responsibility of public officials who believe their government's policy is wrong. To answer these questions is more difficult in that it is as much a matter of judgment as it is of fact. In a Panglossian world, officers should always report what they see, hear, smell, and feel, preferably rounded off with their interpretations and recommendations. If they feel strongly enough and believe they are getting nowhere, their only real choice is resignation. They can, of course, simply report only what they think is expected, an alternative followed by all too many that should speak for itself. There is, however, another middle road that consists of righting from within. If one is battling a strongly held consensus—for instance, when people are bitterly divided on an issue—the odds of winning are negligible. Under Secretary of State George Ball discovered this about Vietnam. President Johnson toyed with him, used him as window dressing, and then ignored him. I happen to have opposed our policies in Vietnam even more strongly than did Ball, but I thought he was deluding himself in the way he went about expressing his opposition. Perhaps ironically, I disagree with his current views on the Middle East, which I think are at least arguable and probably doomed to failure, but he is debating in the open where he has a chance of influencing public opinion and quite possibly of having some official impact. He is still a highly respected man.

Given the passions of the world we live in, and the instinct for survival of most men, it is doubtless unrealistic to hope that anyone other than the occasional oddball or fanatic can consistently live up to an ideal standard. But surely ideals should be held up as a goal for those in public service. There is, however, a danger in oversimplification of very complex issues, and precious few are simple these days. Oversimplification is a malady of the fanatic or of those whose knowledge of the facts and their nuances is strictly limited.

It must be remembered that the reporting out of China in those days, of which Service and Davies were made the scapegoats, gave little heed to the official Washington and the American public to whom it was addressed. For a variety of reasons, neither group wanted to hear or believe what the reporters said. It would have taken a great deal more than a few voices sounding the alarm to have changed a mosaic that had been building up for at least half a century. This is not to say or imply that they should have reported other than they did. To have done so would have been cowardly and a betrayal of the Foreign Service tradition on which we had all been brought up. But it is to say that no one should have been surprised at the reaction to such reporting or to the penalties that were exacted for it. Truth, as in this case, can have dire consequences, and success is a fickle mistress.

To illustrate the hazards, one need only cite the limited postwar planning that was done for East Asia. These plans were based on a few very straightforward assumptions: (1) The China of Chiang Kai-shek's Nationalist government would take its rightful place in the councils of the world as, to use the phrase that was at that time repeated ad nauseam, a strong, united, and democratic China; (2) Japan would be reduced to a strictly agrarian economy; (3) Korea, after a presumably brief trusteeship under the United Nations, would be a free and democratic state; (4) Southeast Asia, apart from a few casual comments by President Roosevelt about the obnoxiousness of a French return to Indochina, would revert to its prewar colonial status; (5) the Pacific Ocean would continue as an American lake. In fact, none of this has really worked out as planned, except for the Philippines, which, despite a few nasty potholes on the road, has not seriously deviated much from the course charted by the Tydings-McDuffie Act of 1934. It may be ironic that the least colonial-minded of all the Western powers turned in the best record. Perhaps President Manuel Quezon had it right when he once commented to me in Washington during World War II, "The trouble with you Americans was that you never brutalized us enough." The recent fall of Ferdinand Marcos and rise of Corazon Aquino in the Philippines, of course, still leaves many questions unanswered.

Clearly, prophecy is an uncertain undertaking, and even reporting has its pitfalls since perspective cannot help but affect outlook. I think one thing that happened during the latter half of this century was a disappearance of civility, the diminution of honest anger into meanness and treachery. Sadly, no one any longer trusts anyone else.

The third set of questions deals with moral and ethical problems and is the most difficult because it is so highly subjective, so much a matter of judgment. What is the relationship of truth to ideology? To foreign policy? To good government? To democracy? If one assumes there is such a thing as an eternal verity, then the easy answer would be the moral trap that without truth nothing has any validity. (I am assuming that the all too prevalent use of torture is an "eternal verity" that is so revolting to all men, except those sick minds who practice it, that it is outside all civilized behavior.) More practically, one can echo Pontius Pilate, that troubled and quite possibly misunderstood man, and ask: What is truth? I am confident that Marx and Lenin, Adam Smith and the National Association of Manufacturers, Confucius, and Lao Tse would have given noticeably contradictory definitions. I qualified "fabrication" before with "not always deliberate" because what may seem like fabrication to me may be no more than my failure to look at the same thing through your eyes.

Whose ox is being gored? If Gandhi is remembered for one thing, it is his insistence on nonviolence under any circumstances, such as calling off the great textile strike in Ahmedabad in the 1920s when violence broke out on the picket lines. And there is also the well-known letter written to him by a woman who asked what he would do if a prowler broke into his house and began to assault his wife and children. He merely noted on the letter which he returned to her: "I expect I would do exactly what you think I would do."

Gladstone, at a time when Islam had reached the nadir of its influence, could brandish a copy of the Koran in the House of Commons and declaim, "As long as a copy of this accursed book survives there can be no justice in the world." He would doubtless have real cause for alarm if he could witness some of the things going on in the Middle East today and their spillover into other people's backyards. But young Muslims who so joyously and casually seek martyrdom have not the slightest doubts about the Will of Allah.

A convinced Communist, and there are a lot of them in this world, believes a lot of things I find extremely distasteful, even untrue. Foreign policy is true or untrue only in terms of the national interests it serves, which may or may not be in conflict with the national interests of someone else. One quarter of the human race in China today lives under a government that is probably as satisfactory to them as any they have ever known, and yet I, born and bred in a western culture, would find it difficult, perhaps impossible, to live in it as a private citizen. Which is truer for whom?

Democracy is probably the least ambiguous of them all. I refer to western style democracy, because many other societies have pilfered the word for their own purposes. Most people in this world have never heard of democracy, but there must be very few people who know anything about it who would not prefer it, even enjoy abusing its opportunities. And if there is any form of social organization in which public truth is essential, it is democracy. Granting the basic commonality of all men and women, as well as their endless and fascinating cultural differences without which life would be very dull indeed, one still must ask, do not all roads lead to and from God?

Perhaps the best and most somber way to end is with Alexis de Tocqueville, who after only nine months in this country in 1831, at the age of only twenty-six, produced the most seminal work on the United States ever written by a foreigner, *Democracy in America.* What is not so well known is that his incredible understanding and foresight about America, written a century and a half ago, are not limited to America. The last page of Chapter XVIII reads as follows:

There are at present two great nations in the world which started from different points, but seem to tend toward the same end. I allude to the Russians and the Americans. Both of them have grown up unnoticed . . . and the world learned of their existence and their greatness at almost the same time. . . . The American struggles against the obstacles which nature opposes to him; the adversaries of the Russian are men. . . . The principal instrument of the former is freedom; of the latter, servitude. Their starting point is different and their courses are not the same; and yet each of them seems marked out by the will of heaven to sway the destinies of half the globe.[10]

Notes

1. Eric F. Goldman, *Rendezvous with Destiny* (New York: Vintage Books, 1956).

2. E. Digby Baltzell, *The Protestant Establishment: Aristocracy and Caste in America* (New York: Random House, 1964).

3. This item from President Reagan is in itself no more than pure trivia, or as he or his spokesmen invariably try to claim, just humor. I include it because the president has an unfortunate habit of making light off-the-cuff or casual remarks with seemingly no thought of what they mean. His staff is obviously embarrassed. If this kind of carelessness were not repeated so often, or the comments were pure humor, that would be one thing. But it is well known that a man's humor is usually a dead giveaway of his basic views and attitudes. This item about Armageddon was so fuzzed over—and so much effort was made to cover it up—that it is difficult to pin down precisely.

4. Professor Robert Newman of the University of Pittsburgh, who probably knows more about the China Lobby than anyone living, is my source for this estimate.

5. Millard Tydings, as cited in David Caute's book, *The Great Fear: The Anti-Communist Purge Under Truman and Eisenhower* (New York: Simon and Schuster, 1978), pp. 36 and 305.

6. The China Lobby: It is astonishing how little has been written about this amorphous group. The first real study was Ross Y. Koen, *The China Lobby in American Politics* (New York: Macmillan, 1960), which as soon as it came out was followed by a letter from the publisher asking all purchasers to return their copies, with assurances a new copy with a corrected introduction would be sent. Naively, since Macmillan has always been a reputable publisher, I complied. Several years of evasive corre-

spondence followed, and I never did get a revised copy. Not until 1974 did Harper and Row publish it again. Macmillan had yielded to China Lobby pressure over a statement in the introduction that Chiang Kai-shek's Kuomintang had been financed by his alliance with the Shanghai underworld. Koen could not document this, even though for decades everyone in Shanghai and almost all foreigners just took this for granted. Not until 1985 has customary documentation been available with the publication by Sterling Seagrave of *The Soong Dynasty* (New York: Harper and Row, 1985). Seagrave has had access to previously unavailable Freedom of Information material. Clearly, some parts of the American government have known much of the story for many years. Also useful is Stanley Bachrack's *The Committee of One Million: The China Lobby in American Politics, 1953–71* (New York: Columbia University Press, 1976).

7. Walter Robinson was assistant secretary of state for Far Eastern Affairs under John Foster Dulles. A Richmond banker by trade and a southern gentleman of the old school, he had served in Chungking as wartime minister-counselor for economic affairs and later in Peiping as head of the Executive Headquarters for General Marshall. He was un-compromisingly pro-Chiang, but unlike some of his cohorts, he was always courtly about it.

8. Barbara Tuchman, *The March of Folly* (New York: Alfred Knopf, 1984).

9. *New York Times,* 12 March 1984. Senator McGovern made this comment in a debate held in Atlanta of the remaining candidates for the Democratic nomination.

10. Alexis de Tocqueville, *Democracy in America*, edited by Richard Heffner (New York: New American Library, 1956 ed.), p. 142.

JOHN W. POWELL

7

The China Hands and the Press: A Journalist's Retrospective

There is an episode in the Bible that comes right after the incident in which Jesus encounters a group preparing to stone a woman caught in adultery. As we all remember, Jesus told the crowd that whosoever was without sin should cast the first stone. Since no one was able to throw the first stone, the project had to be abandoned.

During the spirited exchange which followed between Jesus and the crowd, he told them: "And ye shall know the truth and the truth shall make you free." The discussion continued and the crowd accused Jesus of lying. And Jesus, I presume in some exasperation, finally said: "And if I say the truth, why do ye not believe me?" From there on things rapidly went downhill. By the end of chapter 8 of the Gospel according to John the crowd again picked up its stones, this time to cast at Jesus himself, and he was forced to hide.

A somewhat later historical figure also dealt with the same problem. Mark Twain wrote: "It is by the goodness of God that in our country we have those three unspeakably precious things: freedom of speech, freedom of conscience, and the prudence never to practice either of them."[1]

I think things have improved. American reporters are not normally forced to hide to avoid being stoned—or beheaded, as was the case in ancient China where the emperors often executed the bearers of bad news. But all too often we have been forced to take Mark Twain's advice and become "prudent." Those who have not, especially those of us who covered China several decades ago, have suffered varying degrees of sanction.

I want to spend a moment talking about the men and women who covered China in the 1920s through the 1940s. Many of the early reporters came from Missouri. Some fifty graduates of the Missouri Journalism School went to the Far East, and of these, nearly thirty stayed, mostly in China and Japan. Those who grew to adulthood in the first years of this century, particularly those from the Midwest, were affected by the populism of that period and had a natural sympathy for the underdog, as Akira Iriye discusses elsewhere in Chapter 4.

My father, who was a graduate of the first class at Missouri, refused to ride in a ricksha when he landed in China, firmly convinced that no man should be a beast of burden for another. In later years, whenever circumstances forced him to ride in one, he assuaged his guilt by paying more than the agreed price. This created a new problem as he soon became known to many ricksha pullers—who must have assumed he was the local representative of J. P. Morgan—and they would trot alongside as he walked, making a great fuss as they tried to wheedle him into riding.

Most reporters who stayed and made China their field developed a soft spot for the Chinese people. It was clear that China was seriously put upon. The Western powers had forced numerous unequal treaties on the country at gunpoint. Americans, British, French, and a few other nationals enjoyed and exploited extraterritoriality and were not subject to Chinese law. Some cities, such as Shanghai, Tientsin, and Canton, were treaty ports—foreign enclaves outside Chinese jurisdiction. Foreigners could travel at will to gather news, to proselytize for Christian converts, or to do business, all without a by-your-leave from the Chinese government. These problems, of course, became secondary when Japan invaded China, beginning in 1931 with the occupation of Manchuria and culminating in all-out war in 1937.

The press is supposed to inform the public. It should be a watchdog, exposing injustice and wrongdoing. In addition, the press should be an analyst pointing out the strengths and weaknesses of society. All this is supposed to be accomplished in as objective a manner as possible. Objective reporting from China meant writing about the cruelties of Japanese aggression, revealing the unjustified privileges of the other foreign powers, and, certainly, analyzing the problems and contradictions in Chinese society that contributed to the sorry state in which China found itself.

Over the years, China became more newsworthy in the eyes of American editors, beginning with Sun Yat-sen's Nationalist revolution at the beginning of the century, and especially after the war with Japan began. Thus, more and more American reporters began working in China. They made China their "beat," and over the years became experts or China Hands in their own right. It is not possible to mention all of them or even to discuss the work of more than a handful. Some, such as Edgar Snow, who became justly famous through his writing on China, were best known through their books. Anna Louise Strong, Agnes Smedley, Jack Belden, Graham Peck, Annalee Jacoby, and Teddy White wrote books that have stood up remarkably well. Perhaps the fact that these reporters wrote from the heart gave them extra understanding and perception.

Although the shortcomings of Chiang Kai-shek's Nationalist government were obvious from the beginning of the war with Japan, the main story was the dogged Chinese resistance to the invasion. Despite many incidents of heroism and brilliance on the Chinese side, it soon became a discouraging picture as Chiang steadily retreated before the Japanese. In one of the classic euphemisms of the period, he called it "trading space for time," which ranks right alongside the World War II British descriptions of their retreats as "withdrawals to previously prepared positions." They contrast sharply with General Stilwell's explanation of his defeat in Burma: "We got a hell of a beating." The Chinese capital was moved from Nanking to Hankow and finally to Chungking, a mountain fastness in West China. The war turned into a long stalemate, broken only by occasional Japanese drives, before which Chiang's generals almost invariably retreated. Usually the Japanese eventually withdrew after having looted the area of food and supplies.

With Pearl Harbor in December 1941, the Sino-Japanese War became part of World War II. The American reporters in China suddenly became war correspondents covering one theater of a world war in which their country was now a major participant. The incompetence, corruption, and repressive nature of Chiang's government thus had to be seen in a different light. Nationalist China had become an ally of the United States nearly overnight, and it was the duty of American reporters to point out what a weak reed it was. This was especially important because Pearl Harbor elevated Chiang to near deity status. Perhaps it was national guilt because we had been selling scrap iron and other war materials to Japan. Perhaps it was the stunned, emotional need to believe. In any event, it was widely perceived that Chiang must be a brilliant leader since for four years he had been holding off Imperial Japan, who, we now realized, was a skilled and powerful foe. The Japanese had crippled the American fleet on one Sunday morning and were rapidly overrunning most of Southeast Asia.

It was argued in the United States that sending military supplies to Chiang would produce immediate results because his armies could go on the offensive. The Chinese could fight the Japanese in Asia and for the Americans. Their numbers and leadership could overpower the common foe of Japan.

American correspondents in China found it extremely difficult to disabuse the public of this fantasy. Chiang's government maintained a heavy censorship that deleted even the slightest criticism of his regime. (It is ironic that the acquiescing enforcer of this censorship, and a man who later became Nationalist minister of information, was Hollington Tong, who studied History and Principles of Journalism at Missouri and was one of my father's prize pupils.)

This problem for the reporters was compounded by the issue of communism. Following the Russian Revolution in 1917, a number of Chinese intellectuals turned to Marxism, and from then on there were socialist factions among the various reform groups. Even Sun Yat-sen, in his efforts to unify China, welcomed Communist support. After his attempts to enlist Western aid were rebuffed, he accepted Russian help and incorporated the Chinese Communist Party into his Nationalist movement.

When Chiang took over leadership after Sun's death, the Nationalist-Communist alliance was at best strained and eventually erupted into a civil war. (This is the story that Edgar Snow told so well in *Red Star Over China*.[2]) There was a temporary reconciliation—a United Front between Nationalists and Communists—during the initial period of resistance to the external threat of Japan's invasion, but it soon collapsed.

A few other reporters and observers had managed to follow Snow's footsteps and had slipped into the Red-controlled areas. Most brought back reports confirming Snow's assessment of the Chinese Communists. Despite the spartan existence—Chiang had the Communists bottled up in a remote, barren region in the Northwest—the Communist areas were an oasis of purity in comparison to Chiang's Kuomintang sinkhole.

Moreover, the Communists also had been forced to retreat in the face of the Japanese onslaught, but they had left small units and organizers behind who, in alliance with the peasantry in the areas abandoned to the Japanese, had formed rural guerrilla detachments that harassed Japanese outposts and communication lines. This development posed a dilemma for Chiang. The Communist guerrillas were spread throughout almost all of the Japanese-occupied areas. Every square mile he gave up to the Japanese was soon infiltrated by the Communists and Chiang was unable to match them with guerrilla forces of his own because his oppressive regime had long since alienated the peasants, who were the backbone of the guerrilla operation.

As a number of these veteran reporters, including Arch Steele, one of the more thoughtful correspondents in China during those days, noted in a discussion at Arizona State University:[3] How were the reporters going to explain to a generally anti-Communist America that our Chinese Nationalist allies were hopelessly corrupt and virtually useless in the war against Japan, while the Chinese Communists were providing better quality government in their areas and were also actively harassing the Japanese? Aside from being a difficult story to write, it was nearly impossible to get such accounts through Nationalist censorship. Nevertheless, dispatches occasionally were hand-carried by travelers leaving China. But even then the story was not fully told. It was not unusual for the dispatches of Annalee Jacoby of *Time* magazine and Mac Fisher of United Press to be altered significantly by editors at home as they turned fact into fiction. Annalee once found one of her interviews barely recognizable, for her editor actually had inserted many fictional questions and answers into the piece for publication.

Whittaker Chambers, the ex-Communist who recently was posthumously awarded the Medal of Freedom by President Reagan, was the foreign editor of *Time* during this period and regularly doctored the dispatches of Annalee Jacoby and Teddy White from China and those of John Hersey from Moscow. In this he was given a free hand by his boss, Henry Luce, a close friend and intensely strong supporter of Chiang Kai-shek. When Hersey complained to Luce, he told him he felt Chambers was doing a good job.

Correspondents for the major newspapers did not have this problem. The *New York Times*, for example, ran their correspondents' stories as received. However, as Israel Epstein, who has investigated a study of the *Times* coverage of China, has pointed out, the headline was sometimes in contradiction to the story, which led to reader confusion.[4] So, despite the best efforts of an able press corps in China, the American public was at best inadequately informed and at worst misinformed.

As we know, a parallel situation existed for the U.S. Foreign Service officers, or China Hands, stationed in China. They, too, had to report the unwelcome facts to Washington. Official policy was to support Chiang Kai-shek, however, and such reports were not only disquieting but, in effect, challenged the very wisdom of our foreign policy.

General Stilwell, whose mission was to organize Chiang's armies to fight the Japanese, found the task virtually impossible. When American arms and munitions arrived for his armies, they disappeared into the hidden stockpiles Chiang was hoarding for a resumption of the civil war against the Communists once the United States had defeated Japan. When Stilwell got Chinese troops into Burma and India, where Chinese officials could not "requisition" their supplies, he molded them into an effective force. However, he had to fight and plead with Chiang—often in vain—to let him put them into action against the Japanese. Chiang did not want to risk losing them because he planned to use them, too, in the postwar civil war with the Chinese Communists.

Stilwell became convinced that if he could get arms to the Chinese Communist troops they would make more of a contribution to the war effort than the Nationalists. Understandably, Chiang totally opposed this plan and worsening relations eventually led to Stilwell's recall. The American government was wedded to the Chinese Nationalists.

By removing the Japanese threat, the end of World War II saw a resumption of the Chinese Civil War. Wartime censorship was over, so the press could report the facts. But, once again, Chiang

Kai-shek's corruption and his looming defeat by the Communists were not what America wanted to hear. Washington was particularly sensitive to the bad news since the United States had become heavily involved in the Civil War, supplying Chiang with arms and military advisers and also operating an extensive Nationalist troop training program. Supporting Chiang's despotic regime was not only morally wrong, it was politically stupid, as the China Hands continually attempted to point out. Mao Tse-tung and Chou En-lai long ago had asked to come to Washington to talk things over, but the invitation was never extended. Washington was in a straitjacket largely of its own making.

As is so often the case when a policy fails, instead of realistic analysis, there is a search for scapegoats. The Cold War and McCarthyism made this almost inevitable and those who had not been prudent and who had been the bearers of bad news became the victims of the witch-hunt.

The stories of several of the main China Hands actors are discussed throughout this book. But I want to briefly tell the story of two lesser-known figures in this drama: an American named Mac Fisher and a Chinese by the name of Liu Tsun-chi.

Mac Fisher was the United Press correspondent in Chungking at the time of Pearl Harbor. Shortly thereafter the American ambassador persuaded Mac to head an official information service in China, which later became the Office of War Information. Chris Rand and I, and a number of others, were sent out from Washington early in the war to help Mac. When we arrived, he already had a fairly decent operation going. He had hired some Americans, such as Graham Peck, locally and had put together a good Chinese staff.

Heading it was an extremely able young Chinese newspaperman named Liu Tsun-chi. He worked for the Office of War Information throughout the war, and in the early postwar period came to the United States on a fellowship. He returned to China, worked for a while with the successor organization, the United States Information Service, and then returned to Chinese newspaper work.

When the Chinese Civil War ended, Liu became an information official in the new Communist government. And, as I learned later, he was one of a group of modern Chinese newsmen who urged reform of the old style Chinese journalism. At the end of World

War II, Mac Fisher continued working for the American government as an information specialist in the State Department.

When Senator McCarthy attacked the State Department, claiming that subversion within the department had caused the United States to "lose" China, State caved in and agreed to conduct a loyalty investigation of its employees. The investigators eventually came to Mac. He had been an important figure in the wartime American establishment in China. Was it possible that he had been a secret Communist sympathizer? After all, he had hired Liu Tsun-chi as his chief Chinese editor and Liu had later become an important official in the Communist government.

It would have been impossible for Mac, or anyone else, to have explained to Senator McCarthy that almost the entire Chinese intellectual establishment had eventually opted for the Communist side in the civil war. Years of bad government had lost the Nationalists the support of the peasants, the middle class, and the intellectuals. The country was run by and for a feudal elite whose only solution to the nation's problems was to return to the Confucian verities and inequalities of the past.

In the months that followed, Mac covered page after page of earlier notes and dispatches, putting down his thoughts, searching his memory for explanations of every major act during the previous half dozen years. Agony, accusation, and suspicion followed. After many months, he finally was cleared—sort of. It was accepted that he was not a Communist, but there were still some unresolved doubts—at least, for instance, he was thought guilty of poor judgment. He wasn't fired, but sent away to an obscure post in Turkey and eventually brought back, and then barred from ever holding any important policy-making position again.

In the mid-1950s the Chinese Communists launched the first of their own witch-hunts. Liu was brought up on charges of subversion and disloyalty. It was a fact that he had worked for the American government and was known to be friendly with many American newsmen. It was also known that he had worked closely with the American imperialist agent, Mac Fisher. Liu was labeled a "rightist," fired from his job, and sent to a forestry camp for "labor reform." After a few years he was released from the labor camp and assigned to an obscure interior post as a librarian. Shortly thereafter, Mao launched the "cultural revolution," and Tsun-chi was hauled back to Peking for further examination. This time he went to prison. Altogether, he spent some twenty years in exile and in disgrace.

I saw Liu in Peking just a few years ago. He has been rehabilitated and is now the editor of *China Daily*, the English-language paper published by the Chinese government. And again, he is one of the leaders in an effort to reform Chinese press practices, to promote investigative journalism, and give Chinese reporters more freedom to function as their society's watchdog.

The tragedy goes beyond the ruined careers of Mac Fisher, an American who understood China, and Liu Tsun-chi, a Chinese who understood America. If irrationality had not prevailed, they, and many others like them on both sides, might have succeeded in lessening the hostility between China and America and the estrangement would not have lasted for nearly twenty-five years. If this had been the case, we might have avoided two costly and futile wars on the Asian mainland, one in Korea and the other in Vietnam.

In my case, it was McCarthyism and the Korean War that caused problems. When my wife and I returned from China, U.S. Customs officials in San Francisco confiscated my library on the grounds that it was illegal to import anything from China. I pointed out that most of the more than 1,500 volumes were published in the United States and England and had been taken to China by my father and me over a period of many years. I finally hired a lawyer.

We had a number of exasperating sessions with Collector of Customs Chester MacPhee. I complained that even the New Testament was being held. Initially Customs ruled that no book, including the New Testament, could enter the United States if it had physically been to Communist China. Later, MacPhee said that the real problem was that there was a lot of "Communist propaganda" among my books. In a sense this was true. I had collected practically everything I could find that the new Chinese regime had published: books, pamphlets, and posters. But it was hardly "a lot" and constituted only a small portion of the total.

The collector suggested—without making any promises—that we go through the library, segregating the "political" from the "nonpolitical." Fortunately, I had a list of all the books, prepared at the insistence of the Chinese Customs as a condition of getting them out of China. (The Chinese had removed about 200 books before

I left and it took almost four years of negotiations to get them released.)

My lawyer, a very bright young woman, and I decided to stand on principle and refused to participate in a screening of the titles. She also suggested that as a practical matter such a process might be difficult. For example, she said as she glanced through the list, "How do you feel about Thomas Hardy's *Jude the Obscure?*" MacPhee seemed stumped and turned to an aide: "O'Reilly, what about *Jude the Obscure?*" O'Reilly sat for a bit, then said: "Well, there are some questionable passages." The library was finally released in 1961, but only on the condition that I pay storage charges. Compared with other problems my wife and I later had, the library seizure was a minor matter.

I was called before the U.S. Senate Internal Security Subcommittee. This was a traumatic experience—indeed my worst. I thought I was prepared for it, but it soon became evident that I was not. Perhaps there really is no way to prepare.

I had written a statement setting forth my views on American Far Eastern policy that I planned to read into the record. However, Senator William E. Jenner (Rep. Indiana), the chairman of the subcommittee, told me I should have submitted it earlier and now could not use it. I complained, and he said to leave it and perhaps it would become part of the record. It must have gone into the wastebasket as it was not included in the published record of the proceedings.

The hearing was not like one in a court of law, although the formal trappings were similar. The proceedings began with a series of witnesses, few of whom I recognized and most of whom I had never known. They were asked questions such as "Do you know this man?" and "What do you think of him?" The responses would be something like, "Yes, I know him and he is a Red. He probably is receiving money from China and Russia." Some rambled on at length, reporting hearsay and gossip. Cross-examination was not permitted.

Eventually I was called to testify. Questions were often long and leading and, from me, Senator Jenner usually demanded a "yes" or "no" answer. In one instance, he asked me a have-you-stopped-beating-your-wife type question and I complained, saying that I could not possibly be asked such a question. He immediately shouted: "That's an answer! Let the record show that the witness was unable to respond to even a simple question!"

I gave up and followed my lawyer's advice, refusing to answer questions, citing the First Amendment guarantee of freedom of the press and speech. The senator said he "did not recognize" the First Amendment and I had to settle for the Fifth Amendment's provision that a citizen cannot be compelled to be a witness against himself.

It was very difficult to use the Fifth Amendment because Senator Jenner would periodically add: "Let the record show that this witness is not cooperating with the Senate of the United States in the exercise of its lawful duties, and apparently feels that a truthful answer to the Committee's questions would indeed incriminate him." Occasionally he would vary the statement, saying " . . . would expose him to prosecution for violating the laws of the United States." You can imagine what the next day's headlines were like!

Senator Jenner kept up the pressure, and my wife and I and a colleague were subsequently indicted for sedition. It was claimed that our reporting on the Chinese Revolution and the Korean War had been false and was designed to cause harm to the United States. The total possible penalty was two hundred and sixty years imprisonment and a fine of $130,000.

My favorite of the thirteen counts of the indictment was one that said that I had written that the Chiang Kai-shek government was a corrupt regime and a pawn of the United States. I would not have minded going to trial on that one. However, the prosecutors apparently had second thoughts and withdrew it.

Most of the charges concerned the Korean War. I had reported that it was primarily a civil war, that the United States was behaving aggressively, that the "carpet bombing" of North Korea was genocide, and that the Chinese charges of U.S. use of biological warfare were well founded. Based upon conversations with Chinese reporters, physicians, and scientists, and a reading of the documentary evidence, I believed the charges were true, and still do.

There was a mistrial after one week of testimony, but the prosecutor stated he would seek a new trial and also filed a complaint of treason. Thus we had treason added to sedition! However, the grand jury failed to return an indictment and the judge dismissed the treason complaint. The sedition charge was eventually dropped in 1961 at the request of Robert Kennedy, who had become the new attorney general.

Because I wrote critically—indeed harshly—of America's China policy and of my country's role in the Korean War, we had seven difficult years. They were frightening, time-consuming, and horribly expensive. What we should remember from all of this is that ignorance is costly and that those who try—and sometimes succeed—in shaping the news to fit their own narrow interests do their countries a great disservice.

Notes

1. Mark Twain, *Following the Equator*, vol. 1 (New York: Harper & Brothers, 1899), p. 198.

2. Edgar Snow, *Red Star Over China* (New York: Grove Press, 1961), originally published in 1938.

3. A conference entitled "War Reporting: China in the 1940s" was sponsored by Arizona State University and directed by Steve MacKinon in 1982. It is discussed briefly in print by James C. Thomson, Jr., "China Reporting Revisited," and Walter Sullivan, "The Crucial 1940s," in *Nieman Reports*, XXXVII (Spring 1983):30–34.

4. Israel Epstein, as conveyed in discussions during the conference cited in ibid.

8

The China Hands' Experience: Journalists and Diplomacy

Not long after he arrived in China's wartime capital as an envoy of President Roosevelt in the fall of 1944, Major General Patrick J. Hurley asked a young *Time* magazine correspondent, Annalee Jacoby,[1] to help him get acquainted with high-ranking officials in the Nationalist government. Hurley, a tall, bluff, blustery Oklahoman, was in Chungking to negotiate Lend-Lease agreements and, more importantly, to find a way to get the Nationalists and the Communists to work together in prosecuting the war against the Japanese and to forge a coalition government that would end China's long civil war. Would the reporter, he asked, be willing to arrange a banquet at Hurley's house and be on hand to introduce him to his guests?

Jacoby agreed to help. "Looking very chic" (she recalled wryly forty-one years later) wearing her Army-issue raincoat over a "battered" evening gown, she joined the handsome, white-haired envoy on the appointed evening and dutifully introduced him to his guests, who included Foreign Minister T. V. Soong, other cabinet ministers, a half-dozen generals, and their wives. "The dinner went off swimmingly," with much toasting and gaiety, Jacoby recalls, until the elderly American emissary rose wet-eyed to toast his wife, "my tall, blonde goddess of a bride." To the embarrassment of his guests, he raised his glass to Jacoby, confusing the five-foot-three, twenty-seven-year-old brunette with his much older, taller, and lighter-haired wife whom he had left behind in the United States. As the journalist squirmed in her chair, Hurley "reminisced about our wedding night,"

Jacoby said. "He was talking to *me!*" When the guests had gone, she told the general, "For a little while, you didn't know where you were." Hurley, who in only a few weeks would become the U.S. ambassador to China at one of the most critical junctures in the two nations' joint history, nodded. "Sometimes," he admitted, "I'm in Oklahoma."[2]

To the stunned correspondent, the incident suggested that Roosevelt's envoy was senile, or becoming so, and she reported as much to George Atcheson, the chargé d'affaires at the American embassy. But it was not the kind of story she could report to American readers back home. There was, after all, a war on, and patriotic reporters did not cavalierly question the competence of American leaders on the basis of evidence that would surely be disputed. And there was another reason for not reporting the story. "If she had, she would have been thrown out of the country," said Robert "Pepper" Martin, a United Press correspondent in Chungking at the time.[3] The Kuomintang would not hesitate to invalidate the credentials of a correspondent whose story would, in the words of the chief censor, "disturb the cordial relationship" between the United States and China.[4] Had she been able to sneak the story past the censors, Jacoby's editors at *Time* would almost certainly not have used it on grounds it would undermine the American war effort and U.S. policy in China as interpreted by the magazine's powerful owner and publisher, Henry Luce. Partisans of the Nationalist government, Luce and his editors had already altered or killed numerous dispatches that criticized the Kuomintang, cast the Communists in too favorable a light, or otherwise seemed to question the wisdom of American support of Chiang Kai-shek. Jacoby and her colleague, Theodore H. White, would have to leave China and *Time* magazine before they could write about Hurley as they really saw him and about the situation in China as they felt it really was.

Hurley, of course, went on to become the architect of what some historians believe was a colossal American foreign policy disaster— the failure to achieve an accommodation between the Kuomintang and the Communists during the last months of World War II, and— even more important—the subsequent decision to extend America's hand only to Chiang Kai-shek's corrupt regime and reject the friendly overtures of a Communist government that most American reporters and diplomats believed to be more efficient, honest, egalitarian, and popular. As White and Jacoby wrote in their postwar book, *Thunder out of China*, the United States "chose to prove to the Chinese Communists that no matter how friendly they might be to us, we would support the government of Chiang Kai-shek against them under any circumstances."[5] That misjudgment, it can be argued, helped create the political climate that spawned the Korean and Vietnam wars.

Ill-informed, confused, and naive, Hurley "just couldn't get Chinese politics straight," Jacoby contends, and his bizarre diplomatic behavior—flying unannounced into Communist headquarters at Yenan and greeting his surprised hosts with Choctaw war whoops—made things worse.[6] When his negotiations to form a coalition failed, he accused his own advisers and other Americans at the scene of pro-Communist behavior that had subverted his mission. Hurley was the first to make the cruel and irresponsible charges that sullied reputations and destroyed careers of the Foreign Service officers and journalists who are the subjects of this book. Before White left China in 1945, the distinguished *Time* correspondent would hear himself denounced by the U.S. ambassador as "un-American" and as a "seditious little son of a bitch."[7]

Jacoby believes her anecdote about Hurley—"that poor, befuddled old man"—explains much about American diplomacy in China during those last crucial months of World War II.[8] But the story—and the circumstances that prevented her from reporting it—also suggests much about the journalists who covered China during and after the war, their extraordinary relationship with American diplomats, and the complicated and contradictory world in which they worked.

The China-based journalists were, as John Hohenberg wrote in his study of foreign correspondents, "a distinguished group."[9] They included two eventual Pulitzer Prize recipients and two future Harvard Nieman Fellows. Quartered for the most part in the Press Hostel in Chungking, they included White, a precocious Harvard man whose incisive reporting from China for *Time* and *Life* would gain wide attention in America and who would later win a Pulitzer Prize for his book, *The Making of the President—1960*; A. T. Steele of the *Chicago Daily News*, a highly respected veteran who would eventually be regarded as the dean of American correspondents in the Far East; F. Tillman Durdin of the *New York Times*, described by Hohenberg as "one of the wisest and most experienced correspondents

in Asia" and by White as "a man of such integrity that even Chinese
government officials flinched when they lied to him"; Brooks Atkinson,
Durdin's *New York Times* colleague who left his position as drama
critic to become a wartime correspondent in China and who would
go on to Moscow where his reporting would win a Pulitzer; and
Jack Belden of International News Service, a gutsy, adventurous
idealist whose superlative eyewitness account of General Joseph
Stilwell's retreat out of Burma earned him recognition as one of
the best combat reporters of World War II and whose excursions
into Communist-controlled China made him one of the few correspondents with firsthand knowledge of political and military developments in those areas.

Except for Atkinson, who was in his mid-forties, the individuals
who interpreted events in China for American readers were in their
twenties and thirties. Bright, idealistic, and adventurous, they were
drawn to China by their urge to be at the scene of world-shaking
events they could only read about in college. White, a summa cum
laude history graduate from Harvard, left Boston in 1938 to satisfy
"my absolute lust to see what was happening in the China I had
studied" and to answer the question, "How *did* history actually
happen?"[10] Steele, who had grown up in Toronto and Salt Lake
City and graduated from Stanford with a degree in economics and
journalism, was going broke running a weekly newspaper in California
when news reached America in 1931 that Japan had invaded
Manchuria. Deciding "this is my chance" to become a foreign
correspondent, he sailed for Shanghai on a Japanese freighter "with
$200 in my pocket and no prospects in hand."[11]

Jacoby, who had studied psychology and edited the college daily
at Stanford before taking a job in Hollywood as an MGM scriptwriter,
read about the bombings in Chungking in 1941, thought China
sounded "fascinating and heroic," and wangled an assignment with
United China Relief that paid part of her ticket to Asia on a Norwegian
freighter.[12] Hugh Deane recalls "getting the China bug" when he
attended the University of Lingnan in Canton as an exchange student
from Harvard in 1938. Determined to go back, he talked the *Christian
Science Monitor* into hiring him as a stringer in China.[13] Durdin,
burning to see what lay beyond Texas Christian University and the
West Texas plains where he had grown up, got a deckhand's job
in 1930 on an outbound freighter in Houston and made his way

around the world to Shanghai, where he jumped ship and was hired by an English-language newspaper, the China Press.[14] Robert Martin, a native of Oakesdale, Washington, earned an economics and journalism degree from the University of Washington and served apprenticeships with Pasco and Seattle newspapers before joining the United Press. "Eager to go to China," he got his wish in 1938 when he was sent to Shanghai.[15]

Durdin and Steele came to Chungking with the most experience. Both had roamed widely throughout China in the 1930s, coming together occasionally to cover the most important events of the Sino-Japanese war. Friendly competitors, they were the only two American correspondents to cover the fall of Nanking in December of 1937, and they escaped from the city together on an American gunboat that had just picked up the survivors of the Panay, the U.S. vessel that had been strafed by Japanese warplanes. "Somehow," Durdin recalls, "Steele got his story out before our gunboat reached Shanghai. He never told me how." Forty-eight years later, Steele still will not say how he scooped his colleague. "It's kind of interesting," he said, "but it's probably better not talking about it. Let's just say I was lucky."[16]

When the retreating Nationalist government established Chungking as its capital, the American correspondents followed. Situated between the Yangtze and Chialing rivers on a wedge of high land that overlooked the vast distances of farmland in the remote Szechwan province of south-central China, the city had only 200,000 inhabitants when the Nationalist government arrived in 1938, but by 1940 nearly a million inhabitants were crowded behind its ancient walls.[17]

To the idealistic young Jacoby, who arrived in 1941, Chungking seemed a reporter's dream. In the face of a seemingly unstoppable Japanese invasion force, Chiang Kai-shek was continuing to direct his country's stubborn resistance. Enemy bombers were pounding the city relentlessly, devastating the mud and bamboo dwellings, and killing or wounding thousands of residents who were unable to reach the safety of the cliffside caves above the Yangtze. Yet the resilient Chinese emerged each day from the shelters with undaunted spirit and renewed determination to rebuild their city and drive the invaders from their country. For American journalists in Chungking, it was an inspiring scene. "We revered those people," Jacoby recalls. More than four decades later, she remembers vividly the "hard-working Chinese officials, their faces shining with hope and joy. Those first years in Chungking were the most wonderful of our lives," Jacoby said. "We might be starving, but we were so idealistic at the beginning. We felt very strongly that we were in touch with great things."[18]

The image of China evoked by those wonderful early years would be a difficult one for reporters to dispel once the situation had changed. White and Jacoby wrote in *Thunder out of China:*

> Looking back on Chungking across the years that succeeded Pearl Harbor, it seems strange now to speak of it in such terms of enthusiasm. By the end of the war it had become a city of unbridled cynicism, corrupt to the core. But the early Chungking, under the bombings, was more than a legend that foreign correspondents told the world. The foreigners who lived with the Chinese were caught up in the spirit of the place and swept away by it. From them the illusion of a great and vibrant China made its way across the world, and by the time Pearl Harbor imposed new standards of restraint and censorship, the picture was fully established, and it was difficult to write of the changes that were falsifying it. Toward the end of the war, when censorship was lifted and a more truthful view of Chinese politics began to be given the American people, the facts were so at variance with the illusion generated out of Chungking's early ordeal that the outside world came to believe that the city's spirit had always, even in the beginning, been a propagandist's lie.[19]

After previous accommodations had been flattened by bombs, the Chinese Ministry of Information built a Press Hostel for foreign correspondents next to the ministry on the site of an old grammar school. Situated on high ground above the Yangtze, the thatch-roofed, bamboo and mud structure was "quite pretty," Jacoby said. It would eventually have two stories, with a wooden balcony walkway and a small triangular interior garden where a gardener tended a banana palm tree and clipped the grass with scissors. But it was hardly luxurious—oiled paper served as window glass, a precaution against bomb concussions, and there was no running water. The correspondents shared a couple of bathrooms, each equipped with a rough concrete toilet and bathtub, the latter kept full of cold, brown river water whose sediment formed a thick layer of mud on the bottom. Using a tin washbasin, the reporters bathed themselves, then poured the used water down the toilet. Each sleeping room had a small charcoal stove made from an American oilcan. A separate dining room—the Press Hostel mess—offered "limited cuisine," Deane recalls.[20]

At first, the American correspondents constituted only a small group—representatives of the Associated Press, United Press, International News Service, *Time*, the *Chicago Daily News,* the *New York Times,* and a couple of free-lance reporters. They were joined by correspondents for the French news agency, Havas, which later became Agence France Press; the British news service, Reuters; and two German news agencies. By 1944, the group had grown to forty or fifty.

The reporters were, as Deane recalls, "a politically mixed bag," making for lively discussions over dinner.[21] On the right were the German correspondents, whose pro-Nazi point of view was pronounced. On the left were Belden, Deane, Guenther Stein of the *Christian Science Monitor*, and freelancers Anna Louise Strong and Agnes Smedley. Idealistic, impassioned, and sympathetic to the Communist perspective, they were regarded by their colleagues as serious and responsible journalists in spite of their political views. Though not universally liked, Stein was conscientious and thorough. He was "a beaver, by God," when he was researching a story, recalls China Hand John Stewart Service, based in Chungking at the time.[22] Though Smedley and Strong made no pretense at being objective journalists, few of their colleagues begrudged them that. Smedley was "well-liked—well-loved," recalls Steele. "We respected her," he said, "because she had better contacts with the Communists than we did." Yet, Steele adds, her advocacy made it "unthinkable to repeat her stuff."[23] When China Hand John Paton Davies once cautioned Smedley "not to commit herself so totally" to the Communist point of view, she reportedly answered: "I can't—there is no other way for me."[24] Strong was also "a total advocate," recalls John W. Powell, who worked for the U.S. Office of War Information in China and later as a newspaper journalist. "She really had her heart in it—a woman of the people. She was always defending the underdog, whether he needed it or not."[25]

Though there was not general agreement among the journalists about the political situation in China, the majority preferred the

Kuomintang to the Communists. "They were politically very skeptical of the Communists, even though they saw the faults of the Kuomintang," Deane maintains. "Most of the journalists were in the center. They did their best to provide a balanced account." In this category were reporters like Durdin, Chris Rand of the *New York Herald Tribune*, Robert Martin, Mac Fisher and Al Ravenholt of the United Press, Spencer Moosa of the Associated Press, Dick Potter of the *Baltimore Sun* and Steele, whom Deane sees as "the epitome" of the evenhanded reporter. The journalists on the left and those in the center were linked by a common affection and respect for Edgar Snow, the venerable reporter whose book, *Red Star over China*, had introduced the world to the Chinese Communists in the 1930s. Though some reporters thought he had gone overboard in his sympathetic portrayal of the Communist movement, Snow's reportorial skills, his integrity, and his understanding of China "set a kind of standard," Deane says, for those who followed.[26]

It was only natural that the reporters and Foreign Service officers in Chungking should become well acquainted. Both groups included an unusually high percentage of intelligent, well-informed, and energetic young Americans who were all striving toward the same end—trying to find out what was going on in China. The city's Western community was small enough so that it was all but impossible for its members not to mix socially as well as professionally. The result was an extraordinarily close and harmonious relationship between journalists and diplomats—a relationship, Steele believes, that was "freer and more open" than the ones he experienced in other parts of the world during his long career as a foreign correspondent.[27]

"We had a common interest—to get at the facts and the truth," says Durdin. "I thought the facts and the truth were guiding American policy in those days."[28] Certainly journalists could identify with the goal of the Foreign Service officer as expressed by Raymond Ludden, a Chungking-based diplomat: "to report the truth as he sees it, without adjusting it to American domestic considerations."[29] When the reporters were asked in 1985 to single out their colleagues who did the best "reporting" in China, they revealingly mentioned Foreign Service officers Service and Davies in the same breath as Steele, White, and Durdin.

"From the day I arrived in China I learned that the embassies and consulates were where I got a lot of useful information," Steele recalls. "The diplomats had to be consulted if the story was to be covered. Often they were privy to a much higher level of intelligence than we had."[30] Most of the correspondents were not steeped in Chinese history nor could they speak the language fluently, much less read the newspapers. But the embassy had individuals who could, and would, share their knowledge and language skills.

"It was," recalls Durdin, "a very open and constructive relationship on both sides." The diplomats liked to try their stories out on the correspondents, while the reporters would seek validation of their information from the embassy people. "We often traded our news for their news," Steele said. "It was a fair exchange, but I think we used the diplomats more than they used us." Service saw his relationship with journalists in a similar light. "I was a source and they were a source," he said.[31]

By today's journalistic standards, such a liaison might appear to be improper—getting so close to your source as to endanger the reporter's impartiality. But nothing in the relationship "could have been construed as unethical or improper" given the circumstances, Steele argues. "I don't think we lost our judgment."[32] Most of the journalists and diplomats consulted for this chapter agree. "You have to understand the context of the time," says Durdin. "There was not the official concern with secrecy and there were no inhibitions about the State Department then. Their people were much more candid and open in those days. I felt no conflict in my relationship. I told them whatever information I had obtained. Well, usually."[33] Martin, the United Press correspondent in Chungking who went on to a distinguished career with *U.S. News and World Report*, believes that he was never intentionally misinformed by a Foreign Service officer in China. There were times, however, when he felt he had been given erroneous information, and then he simply disregarded it.[34]

Given their common sense of purpose, it was not surprising that a reporter like Jacoby would agree to arrange a banquet for a visiting envoy like Hurley. Neither Hurley's request nor Jacoby's acceptance would be thought, under the circumstances, "particularly out of line," believes Steele.[35]

Though Kuomintang officials were relentless censors of foreign news dispatches, the American diplomats who monitored the news media were less disposed to be heavy-handed, particularly with reporters they had gotten to know. When attaché David Barrett instructed Hugh Deane of the *Christian Science Monitor* not to report a particular story, "I simply didn't pay any attention," Deane said. Nothing came of it. This is not to say, however, that sparks did not fly occasionally when American national security clashed with notions of journalistic responsibility. Service recalls censoring part of a New *York Times* story written by Brooks Atkinson. "He was damn mad," Service recalls with a chuckle.[36] Yet the Foreign Service officer, who considered Atkinson "an unusually gifted reporter," risked his career a few months later by helping the correspondent smuggle out his explosive story detailing how Chiang Kai-shek had forced the recall of General Joseph Stilwell, the highest-ranking American in China. The story, as historian Barbara Tuchman wrote, would "blow the roof" off Kuomintang censorship and unleash a barrage of news stories criticizing Chiang's regime.[37]

Service's willingness to share his information with journalists eventually got him into trouble. When, in 1945, police raided the offices of the pro-Communist magazine, *Amerasia,* they found copies of the diplomat's reports from Yenan in the files. In an effort to inform the press, Service had lent the drafts of the reports to the magazine's editor. "Jack Service felt things very strongly and was very much disturbed by the situation in China," Steele says. "He acted out of conscience. I haven't the slightest belief that he had any Communist connection. He may have been unwise in turning those things over, however. I respect his emotion in the matter; as to his judgment, that's another thing."[38] Service himself agrees that his behavior was "indiscreet."[39]

It was the Kuomintang, not the American diplomats, who attempted most blatantly to manipulate the press. "The Kuomintang," said Service, "tried to do a snow job—to portray all this as only a brave, historic struggle." White, who worked for the Chinese Ministry of Information before joining *Time,* recalls that his mission was "to manipulate American public opinion" and says flatly that "some of the reporters could be controlled": "The Associated Press was represented by a young Dane with a Chinese wife; Reuters had a Chinese bureau chief; others, too, had given hostages of loyalty to the Chinese government. These reported what the government put out."[40]

Identifying Martin of the United Press and Durdin of the *New York Times* as "the two most difficult reporters to control," White saw visiting big-name reporters as the easiest marks:

Easiest of all to manipulate . . . were the famous names, the trained seals, the swooping stars of big American and British newspapers who could fly in for a four-day visit and then send out pontifical dispatches about the war and the Chinese spirit of resistance. It was with these I had my greatest luck in my brief career as a propagandist; one correspondent arrived in Chungking, was banqueted by the government the evening of his arrival, stayed drunk for his entire four-day visit, lurching from banquet to banquet, and let me, from my desk at the Information Ministry, write all his dispatches.[41]

Though they complained bitterly of Kuomintang attempts to discourage realistic reporting, the American correspondents do not feel they were subjected to similar efforts by American officials until late in 1944, when Patrick Hurley took over as ambassador. In *Thunder out of China*, White and Jacoby reported how the relationship between journalists and the U.S. embassy turned sour. Of Hurley, they wrote: "His fear of the working press became enormous. He imported two personal press attachés and invited visiting correspondents to live with him. The Embassy watched home-going news dispatches to check on the sources of criticism of the ambassador."[42]

Hurley's hostility toward the press notwithstanding, reporters were a useful source of intelligence for American diplomats in China, both during and after the war. The diary of John F. Melby, a Foreign Service officer assigned to Chungking, who also is one of the contributors to this book, contains this entry:

Last night I had a talk with Tillman Durdin of the *New York Times* who had just come back from a visit to Kalgan in the north. According to him the Communists are behaving very well here, being quiet and unobtrusive, and are trying to conciliate the people who are still suspicious and at the same time fear the Kuomintang will come back and wreak vengeance on them if they cooperate in any way with the Communists.[43]

Sometimes it was difficult to determine who was using whom. When Congressman Mike Mansfield was sent to China in 1944 as an envoy of President Roosevelt, he carried a list—supplied in part by the Far Eastern Division of the State Department—of the most knowledgeable journalists and diplomats to consult about the political and military situation in China. His visit with Theodore White was particularly useful. Frustrated by *Time's* tampering with his story about Stilwell's recall, White turned over to the young congressman a copy of his twenty-eight-page, single-spaced letter to Henry Luce, which angrily claimed that the editors had distorted the truth by suggesting that the Kuomintang, though dictatorial, was trying to preserve "the core of democratic ideology against a vicious totalitarian communist dictatorship in the north." White's letter contained a lucid analysis of the strengths and weaknesses of both factions and concluded that though the Communists were the more admirable of the two, the United States at the moment had no other alternative than to continue to back Chiang Kai-shek.

In his reports to the president and to Congress, Mansfield made substantial use of White's observations and analysis. Not only did he borrow White's list of strengths and weaknesses of the Kuomintang and Communists, but he used much of the journalist's language. It was, no doubt, a fair exchange from both White's point of view and Mansfield's. The *Time* reporter was able to get his long-suppressed political and military analysis presented to American leaders and the American public, and Mansfield was able to successfully complete his presidential assignment, gathering precisely the kind of authoritative detail that he needed. His report to Congress would establish him firmly in the public mind as one of that body's most knowledgeable Far East experts.[44]

Some young reporters enjoyed close relationships with Chinese leaders—relationships that raised the eyebrows of more seasoned correspondents. White's autobiography mentions the special friendship he developed over the years with Chou En-lai, whom the reporter revered as a teacher as well as cultivated as a news source. At one point, the Communist leader entertained "Teddy" at a banquet in the journalist's honor "at the finest restaurant in Chungking." The *Time* correspondent no doubt gained special insight into the Communist movement as a result of this relationship, but Chou also got an opportunity to influence, in White's words, "a malleable young American reporter" who worked for a prestigious U.S. magazine.[45]

As Americans whose country was engaged in a "popular" war, the reporters in Chungking were not disposed to report material that would likely give aid and comfort to the enemy. "The word 'patriotism' applies here," said Martin.[46] War correspondents wore American uniforms and enjoyed a measure of trust from military officers and diplomats that would be surprising to the reporters who covered the Vietnam war. When General Stilwell informed White that the United States was allied in China to "an ignorant, illiterate, peasant son of a bitch called Chiang Kai-shek,"[47] he could be sure that the confidence would be respected, whatever its news value. Similarly, American journalists did not rush headlong to expose the bitter behind-the-scenes controversies involving General Claire Chennault and Stilwell or to trumpet their concerns that Chiang Kai-shek was keeping his troops out of combat to save them for the fight with the Communists he knew was coming after Japan's defeat. The impulse was to give American leaders the chance to set things right before going into print with stories that might benefit the Japanese military as much as the American reading public.

Robert Martin recalls hearing Chennault's staff members, angry over Stilwell's unwillingness to devote the brunt of his resources to the air war, suggest sardonically that Chennault send his bombers to flatten Chungking, Stilwell's headquarters, instead of Japanese strongholds. He did not report the comments.[48]

Only once in his career did Martin have strong second thoughts about failing to report an event during wartime. As a correspondent during the Korean War, Martin accompanied a Marine reconnaissance team who captured several Chinese prisoners and shot them on the spot because there was not room in the jeeps for both the Marine wounded and the POWs. The incident took place in September 1950, right after the landing at Inchon, and the fighting had been "very, very bitter," Martin said. The front was "very fluid, and we were five miles beyond what would become the line that evening. I didn't report it," Martin says. "I don't know why. I guess I asked myself, 'What good would this really do?' I wouldn't do it again."[49]

As mutually advantageous as it was, the close relationship between journalists and diplomats could not fail to influence the manner in which events were reported to the American people. Yet there is little agreement today about the nature of that influence. In fact, while right-wing critics have argued that a sinister pro-Communist clique of diplomats and journalists helped America "lose China to the Reds," scholars from the left see the same intimate relationship as contributing to the press' failure to inform the public early enough about the corruption of the Kuomintang regime and the true strength and popularity of the Communists. But the fact that the quality of American reporting in China in the 1940s has been vigorously challenged from opposite ends of the political spectrum suggests that the reporters may have been doing more things right than either camp of critics would care to admit.

It is not hard to see why the coverage should appear, at various stages, to be "pro-Kuomintang" or "pro-Communist." The reporters managed to chronicle the transition of Chiang's regime from the hope and promise of the early years to the despair and cynicism that emerged later as the corruption of the government became increasingly apparent. Late in the war, the correspondents would visit Mao Tse-tung's headquarters at Yenan and conclude that the Communists were better organized, better led, and more in touch with the people than Chiang's government. "What we found," says Steele, "was a revelation—a highly organized society in Yenan, living in caves; a well-disciplined army; a political system that looked democratic."[50]

Ironically, the majority of American journalists had come to China predisposed to be suspicious of Communists. "The conviction of most of us," recalls Steele, "was that Communism was part of a world conspiracy and that Chinese Communism was part of the monolithic movement. That feeling was very strong. But once in China, our feelings got kind of watered down." One of the reasons was that the Communists tended to be better sources of news than the Kuomintang. Durdin and Steele, who had covered the Communists since the 1930s, considered them to be generally reliable news sources. "All of our correspondents had good relations with the Communists," claims Steele.[51] Reporters in Chungking enjoyed easy access to two intelligent and cooperative press liaison officers, Chao Huang-huan and Kung P'eng, and often even to Chou En-lai, who was charming, articulate, and surprisingly open.

On the other hand, the Kuomintang was a "very unreliable source of information," Steele says. Kuomintang press conferences, recalls one journalist who worked for the U.S. Office of War Information in China during the war, were "complete crap."[52] Worse, Chiang's government had established a system of censorship that stopped every dispatch that cast Chiang's government in an unfavorable light. Deane recalls that the censors simply searched the mail—"if they didn't like what you wrote, they put it in a drawer." Hollington Tong, the information minister who had received his college journalism training in the United States, reportedly advocated that correspondents should be barred from visiting the Communists for "humane reasons," because any dispatches they wrote as a result would be censored.[53] Tuchman reports that foreign correspondents grew so angry with the Kuomintang's interference that in April 1944 they addressed a joint request to Chiang Kai-shek, stating that:

> although permitted to send stories that created an idealized portrait of China, they were prevented from writing anything that implied criticism of the government or that disclosed "the full gravity of China's economic situation" or that questioned in any way "the direction, condition or use of Chinese armies," and that it was impossible to function as responsible journalists unless the policy were liberalized. Chiang's answer was merely that reports not detrimental to China's resistance would be given every consideration.[54]

Yet, in spite of the official censorship, Chungking was "a leaker's paradise," said Service.[55] If a reporter really wanted to get a story out, he could send his dispatch with a friend flying out of the country, with instructions to drop it in the mail in Hong Kong. But one did so at the risk of losing accreditation. Late in the war Harold Issacs of Newsweek was barred from China for having written that "Americans will at best find themselves backing a government with no real basis of power except American support."[56]

The Kuomintang was especially energetic in suppressing dissent from Chinese citizens, and American reporters found they had to be careful about getting their Chinese news sources in trouble. After a young writer, Yeh Chun-chiang, took Deane and Belden to interview a dissident economics professor in Chungking, the youth was forced to go into hiding. Deane never saw him again until long after the war, when Ye had become a prominent novelist. "We'd been pretty naive" about exposing Chinese friends to Kuomintang repression, Deane says.[57]

Some American reporters complained that their editors at home altered their dispatches to match their own preconceptions about the situation in China. The degree of interference varied widely, and some reporters had no trouble at all. Durdin recalls that *New York Times* editors never tampered with his dispatches or told him what stories he was to cover. When, as a young reporter, Durdin asked whether he should "stay in Bangkok or go back to China," his editor responded, "How the hell should I know?"[58] Steele enjoyed the same kind of latitude but acknowledges that there were times he was concerned about what his editors would do with his stories, particularly those about the Communists. "Desk people were a bit confused about the coverage coming out of China," Steele recounts. "Reports from the Kuomintang and our reports were contradictory. It was very difficult to cover the story because of the unreliability of either side. The Kuomintang statements couldn't be trusted, and the Communists were always questionable because we had no way of checking them out."[59] Thus, it was not surprising that editors at home played it safe on some stories, balancing reporters' accounts with Kuomintang releases that often were questionable. John Melby's 1945 diary entry suggests how disturbed some newsmen were about the way their dispatches were being handled by their stateside editors: "I had dinner last night with several American newsmen. Apparently like most people here they are violently anti-Kuomintang, speechless about the lack of direction or purpose in American policy, and disgusted with the way their news stories are cut or altered at home."[60]

The most notorious editorial tampering took place at *Time* magazine, where the stories of White and Jacoby were routinely changed to fit Henry Luce's vision of China. As David Halberstam notes, White's excellent reporting from China "would drive him from the Luce publications; White might have his China, but Mr. Luce had his China and he was not going to accept White's version."[61] White's story about the tragic Honan famine of 1943 was an indictment of the Kuomintang's inefficiency, insensitivity, and corruption, but *Time* editors removed details that showed Chiang's government for what it was. Similarly, White's full report about the Stilwell crisis, detailing the general's anger and frustration over Chiang's unwillingness to prosecute the war, was "edited into a lie, an entirely dishonorable story," the Time reporter said.[62] At one point, as E. J. Kahn reports, White grew so frustrated that he hung this sign on his door: "Any similarity between this correspondent's dispatches and what appears in Time is purely coincidental."[63]

Jacoby contends that Whittaker Chambers, who became Time foreign editor in 1945, simply "made up the news" about China. She recalls sending off to New York a long story based on her interview with Chiang Kai-shek, only to see the article completely transformed. "When Time came back over the hump," she says, "there was a six- or seven-page interview story about Chiang, all of it created. Chambers had me asking questions I never asked. He had Chiang answering things he never said. Here was a Time editor writing dialogue for a head of state!" "It was," Jacoby adds, "a perfectly beautiful anti-Communist piece." For reasons such as these, she recalls, "Teddy and I spent more of our time, near the end, arguing with our editors and trying to correct stories than we did actually writing them. We finally both quit—resigned in a fury of indignation."[64]

Today, most of the journalists who covered China during and after World War II vigorously defend the overall accuracy and impartiality of their account. Regarding his disagreement with Luce, White wrote, "I still insist, and know, that I was right and he was wrong in the telling of the story of China."[65] And Steele contends, "We reported things as we saw them. What we saw was that the Kuomintang was in chaotic disarray and the Communists were winning the war. This wasn't pro-Communist reporting. It was objective reporting."[66]

Yet other correspondents question the performance of some of the reporters. "Some of the news," says Durdin, "was too glowing about the Communists and not broad-minded enough about the Kuomintang. The result," he continues, "was an imbalance in coverage" by young reporters who might not have judged the Kuomintang so harshly had they been more experienced. The Chinese, after all, had just emerged from medieval society and were trying to modernize practically overnight. Perhaps no Chinese government at the time was capable of making that transformation without serious problems. Though there was some deliberate slanting of the news, Durdin says, usually it was unintentional. "Some newsmen simply suffered from being over impressed by Chou En-lai," he says. "They didn't put the Communist movement into perspective, but they weren't dishonest. And the fact that the Kuomintang was corrupt was everyday apparent."[67]

Martin agrees that coverage of the Communists may have been too favorable. "We tended to think of them as being definitely more interested in the welfare of the peasants" than they turned out to be, he said. And he wonders whether he and his colleagues might have been unduly influenced by "two very personable individuals in Chungking—Chou En-lai and Chao Huang-huan." Finally, he sees in retrospect that the Communists had an important advantage over the Kuomintang: "When you run a small operation, you're not weighted down by a heavy military bureaucracy."[68]

Steele said his admiration for the Communists cooled considerably after the war. So did Durdin's. Watching "China being torn apart in order for the Communists to create the chaos they needed to take over, I remember telling myself, 'I hope these bastards don't win,'" Durdin recalls. After the Communists took control in 1949, Steele watched official censorship move from mild to severe. When a soldier arrived to inform him there would be no more outgoing mail or telegrams at all, Steele left the country. A few American journalists, like John W. Powell, decided to remain in China. "They were willing," said Steele, "to write articles that weren't very critical of the Communists—they sat on the fence."[69] But if they seemed to Steele to be sitting on the fence, to many Americans they had jumped down into the enemy's pasture.

No American journalist was to suffer more during the McCarthy Era than Powell, who writes of his own experience in this book. His newspaper career, quite simply, was ruined. The son of a prominent American editor in China, Powell grew up in Shanghai. After majoring in journalism at his father's alma mater, the University of Missouri, he worked as a newsman in China and then joined the U.S. Office of War Information at the outset of World War II. After the war, he took over his father's paper in Shanghai, the *China Weekly Review*, and began building a reputation as a serious, conscientious journalist. American reporters characterized him as "fearless" and as one of the best-informed young newsmen in China. An Associated Press article credited him with trying to steer a middle course between the Kuomintang and the Communists.[70]

As one of the few American journalists who stayed in China after the Communists took control, Powell became an increasingly controversial figure in the United States and among his colleagues in the news profession. A hostile *Newsweek* magazine article characterized him, in a headline, as a "Red China Boy."[71] His newspaper was, in fact, sympathetic to the Communist government and highly critical of the Kuomintang. Moreover, he vehemently opposed American involvement in the Korean War and published inflammatory charges that the United States was using germ warfare in that conflict. Although they did not question his integrity or loyalty, some American correspondents who knew Powell felt his reporting was "very biased" and, under the circumstances, injudicious.

When Powell, his wife Sylvia, and their two small children returned home to the United States just after the Korean War, they got a hostile reception. The couple was summoned before congressional committees and asked questions that publicly impugned their loyalty. Then they were indicted by the United States government for sedition and even accused of treason. Korean War POWs testified that Powell's newspaper was required reading as part of the Communist propaganda program imposed on them in prison. Advised by their attorneys not to answer the when-did-you-stop-beating-your-wife questions routinely advanced by their interrogators, the Powells took the Fifth Amendment, an action that suggested to some that they were guilty. "My initial impulse was to argue," Powell recalls. "But this was not a court hearing. They set the rules." If he tried to argue, "they told me to shut up." If he submitted documents as evidence of his innocence, they refused to put them into the record. "They made me look pretty stupid," Powell says. "The Senate Internal Security Subcommittee got some people in Shanghai to testify against me. Some of them I knew, but very few. If I disputed this hearsay, I could be convicted of perjury. In that sense, I was well-advised to answer as little as possible. I took the Fifth, but answered all the same questions later to reporters at the Washington Press Club."[72] It would be years before the charges were finally dropped.

Given the atmosphere of the 1950s, it is not surprising that Powell failed to find a newspaper job when he returned to the United States. He made several attempts, he said, but was told, in effect, "fat chance." He tried to do some freelancing, but was told "I needed a more balanced view of China." Meanwhile Sylvia was dismissed

from her job with the March of Dimes foundation in an action that
was clearly associated with the adverse publicity she and her husband
were getting. Blacklisted, broke, and deeply in debt from his litigation
expenses, Powell read a book on carpentry and began a new career
of fixing up Victorian houses in San Francisco. Eventually the work
grew into a modest antique business that the family still operates
on Church Street. In an effort to clear his name, Powell spent years
poring over government documents he obtained through the Freedom
of Information Act, looking for evidence that would corroborate the
stories about American use of germ warfare during the Korean
War.[73]

Would he, given the hindsight offered by more than three decades,
report anything differently if he had it to do over again? "It's a rare
person who doesn't look over his clips and find something he is
not very happy with," Powell said. "But the basic Korea story is
pretty much what I reported. There is nothing I can find in the
archives that suggests I was off base badly. I would write basically
the same material, but do it more cautiously. I could have saved
myself a lot of trouble by phrasing things somewhat differently."
But he insists that the facts have not changed. "Four postwar years
of the Kuomintang *were* pretty awful," Powell said. "The new
government *was* quite an improvement. Many in the American
community in China agreed with me. We wanted the new government
to be recognized by the United States. But I did not judge the extent
of the Cold War. When we recognized Taiwan, I was enraged."[74]

If Powell is the most controversial journalistic victim of the
McCarthy Era, then White is the most celebrated. *Thunder out of
China*, which was denounced as pro-Communist, helped put him
on the list of those who supposedly "lost China to the Reds." Like
Powell, he would be summoned before a congressional committee,
investigated by the government, and publicly accused of disloyalty.
As a *Time* correspondent, White had acquired a reputation as one
of the ablest and most knowledgeable journalists in Asia. But by
1948 he was unable to find work, "groveling," as he says in his
autobiography, for openings. Because there were no jobs on major
newspapers or magazines for "left-wing writers," White was forced
to accept an undistinguished assignment with a "marginal" news
service. He had become, he says, "an outcast of American journalism."[75] It would take years for him to reestablish his reputation.

The loyalty of other American reporters was also called into question. Henry Lieberman, who covered China for the *New York Times* during the late 1940s, was refused a passport because he had gone to work for the left-wing New York newspaper, *PM.*[76] Jacoby remembers being call a "Communist" and a "Red."[77] One of the few China-based journalists who had the opportunity to cover Senator Joseph McCarthy after the war, Phil Potter of the *Baltimore Sun* recalls that his newsroom files were searched by one of the senator's aides, who has hoping to find evidence that the newsman had once used the sympathetic term "agrarian reformers" to describe the Chinese Communists. The aide was crestfallen when he found only one use of the term—in a statement by Patrick J. Hurley.[78]

For the journalists who served in China during and after World War II, the final irony is that after years of being accused of having been too cozy with the Communists they are now being criticized for being nothing more than press agents of Chiang Kai-shek. Consider Phillip Knightley's scathing indictment of the press:

> In no theatre of the war was the protection of the American public from reality more complete—and in no theatre did it have quite such serious consequences—than in China. There, the reporting of the Sino-Japanese War had created a dangerous myth. This was that the Chinese peasant armies, under the control of their beloved leader, Generalissimo Chiang Kai-shek, and his wife, the beautiful American-educated Madame Chiang Kai-shek, had fought the Japanese to a standstill and that, given American money and military supplies, they could actually defeat them. . . .
>
> In this emotional climate, it would have needed a war correspondent of remarkable calibre to write the truth: that the Chiang Kai-shek regime was massively corrupt, brutal, and inefficient; that Chiang had no intention of pressing the war against the Japanese; that he was stockpiling American military aid to make his rule safe against insurrection. This was not what America wanted to hear; so, instead, correspondents sent the war communiques issued by Hollington K. Tong, and those bore more resemblance to fairy tales than to reality. . . .
>
> They wrote stirring stories about the American Flying Tigers and their leader, Major General Claire Chennault . . . who believed that he could defeat Japan with a hundred or so fighters and fifty bombers . . . They did not write that these opinions brought

Chennault into serious conflict with his superior, General Joseph
Stilwell . . . Nor did they report the bitter breach that grew between
Stilwell and Chiang Kai-shek, because Stilwell knew Chiang for
what he was, an incompetent Fascist commander without the will
to act. . . .[79]

As plausible as Knightley's historical analysis may sound now, it
is hardly fair to blame the journalists of the time for covering up
or for not having seen those conditions with the same measure of
certainty that hindsight provides. Moreover, Knightley shows little
sensitivity to the reality of wartime China, where censors routinely
killed news stories or watered down outgoing dispatches by removing
offensive passages. "It's easy," said Theodore H. White, "for someone
who wasn't there to say thirty years later that we were all being
flacks for Chiang Kai-shek and that we should have violated censorship. We were youngsters—most of us in our 20s. We were
involved in a war. To breach censorship was a violation of the
military code. We didn't do it. We reported what we could, but we
were choked by censorship." Whatever illusions the American people
had about China and its heroic struggle "were spread by American
editors in New York," he added.[80]

Martin, who covered the war in China for the United Press,
acknowledges that American correspondents' coverage of the fighting
in Shanghai and Hankow in the late 1930s might have contributed
to the erroneous idea that the Chinese armies would be the equal
of the Japanese, but beyond that admission he sees no validity in
Knightley's analysis. The scholar, he says, who looks for them will
find that many stories containing criticism of the Kuomintang slipped
past government censorship and made it into print. He points to
several of White's dispatches, which questioned the efficiency and
competence of the Nationalist government, and to two of his own—
one in 1942 that criticized Congress for acquiescing to the "political
blackmail" of Foreign Minister T. V. Soong, who demanded and
received millions of dollars for his country with no safeguards as
to how it would be spent, and another in 1943 that mentioned the
disagreement between Stilwell and Chennault over the priority to
be given to air power in prosecuting the war against the Japanese.
Nonetheless, Martin said, in time of war "you're not going to tell
everything. But almost inevitably all of the warts will show."[81]

Thomas Engelhardt's article, "Long Day's Journey: American Observers in China, 1948–50," is a more scholarly study than Knightley's but is limited to two years. Engelhardt's thesis is one familiar to journalists at least since Evelyn Waugh lampooned foreign correspondents in his novel, *Scoop*, as people who lounge in comfort in the cocktail bars of luxurious hotels as revolutions take place unnoticed. He writes that "When the Kuomintang returned to Shanghai in 1945, foreign newsmen took over the top five floors of the eighteen-floor 'Broadway Mansions.' There, in the 'city's closest approach to a modern American skyscraper,' they set up their correspondents' club, arranged their lodgings and 'danced under gaily colored lights' while 'White Russian mistresses mingled with American wives and both cursed the Chinese.'" Meanwhile, Engelhardt contends, the reporters were missing the fact that in the hinterlands "millions of peasants under the leadership of the Chinese Communist Party had risen with great passion and bitterness, breaking the back of traditional land tenure relationships, often killing the landowners who for so long had controlled their lives." In the countryside, he continues, "the whole structure of Chinese society was being torn apart and put together anew."[82]

A third critique, and the one most germane to this chapter, is offered by Deane, a correspondent who was there. Deane, who gives his colleagues generally high marks for their reporting during this period, raises questions about the relationship between American journalists and diplomats. He argues that correspondents for major newspapers and wire services "wrote dispatches that were shaped by their close, even intimate ties with U.S. diplomats and officers, and certain Kuomintang spokesmen." Those reporters, he says, too often produced "finely balanced accounts of ill-balanced situations"— stories that correctly reported from 1946 to 1949 that the Communists were winning but not that they were also the ones telling the truth.[83]

As an illustration of the tendency of major newspapers to pull their journalistic punches, Deane recalls how the *Christian Science Monitor's* distinguished foreign editor, Charles E. Gratke, chided him for the direct language he used in a series of articles about China in 1941. "When you write for a publication like the *Nation*," Gratke said, "you call a spade a spade. But at the *Monitor* it's a little trowel." Forty-five years after that journalistic lesson, Deane believes that "the little trowel principle" applied a good deal of the time to the coverage of China. Certainly reporters writing for mass-circulation publications or for wire services were likely to be more cautious and evenhanded than those writing for journals of opinion like the *Nation*. Who could blame Jacoby for using the word "petulant" to describe Hurley in *Thunder out of China*, when she really meant "senile"? But Deane believes the aggregate of minced words produced a serious distortion of what was really happening in China in the years immediately following the war:

> The essential reality of the years 1946–49 was a persistent American intervention in China's internal affairs—intervention that only stopped short of the introduction of U.S. armed forces. But in the leading newspapers and news agency dispatches the intervention was never explicit. The unwritten assumption was that the U.S. had the right to do what it was doing. Questions had to do only with practicality. Did this failure later contribute to the acceptance in the United States, at least initially, of the bloody interventions in Korea and Indochina?[84]

It is likely that historians will continue to debate whether American reporters in China were, in fact, too close to their diplomatic sources, and—if they were—whether that made them Communist dupes or Kuomintang flacks. But one suspects that, in the context of the time, a close relationship between journalists and diplomats was inevitable. They needed each other. And the subsequent attacks from both left and right suggest that most of the reporters were pretty close to where they belonged—in the middle.

His criticism notwithstanding, Deane believes that the American reporters in Chungking did a generally good job under extremely difficult circumstances. "China brought out the best in us," he said. "My impression is that the reporting from China was superior to, or as good as, coverage of other foreign situations. Some able people escaped from local universities or jumped ship to serve as journalists. They worked hard and tried conscientiously to get at the facts, and I think attentive readers could have got to the realities from their reports."[85]

Though some acknowledge in hindsight they would do some things differently, the correspondents look back on their work in China with some satisfaction. "Look," says White, "we were sitting on top of a volcano. The top was coming off. We didn't know where it would go. Chiang was going to be exploded out of it." Had he to do it over again, would he change the way he covered those momentous events? His answer: "I wouldn't change one word."[86]

Notes

1. Now Annalee Jacoby Fadiman.

2. Annalee Jacoby Fadiman, Santa Barbara, California, telephone interviews with the author, 16 October and 23 November 1985.

3. Robert Martin, Washington, D.C., telephone interviews with author, 14 December 1985.

4. Theodore H. White and Annalee Jacoby, *Thunder out of China* (New York: William Sloane Associates, 1946), p. 249.

5. Ibid., p. 242.

6. Fadiman interviews.

7. Theodore H. White, *In Search of History: A Personal Adventure* (New York: Harper and Row, 1978), p. 201.

8. Fadiman interviews.

9. John Hohenberg, *Foreign Correspondence: The Great Reporters and Their Times* (New York: Columbia University Press, 1964), p. 370.

10. White, *In Search of History*, p. 55.

11. A. T. Steele, Boise, Idaho, telephone interviews with author, 16 October and 7 and 10 November 1985.

12. Fadiman interviews.

13. Hugh Deane, New York City, telephone interview with author, 23 November 1985.

14. F. Tillman Durdin, San Diego, California, telephone interviews with author, 16 October and 7 November 1985.

15. Martin interviews.

16. Steele and Durdin interviews.

17. White and Jacoby, *Thunder out of China*, p. 8.

18. Fadiman interviews.

19. White and Jacoby, *Thunder out of China*, pp. 8–9.

20. Fadiman and Deane interviews.

21. Deane interview.

22. John Stewart Service, Berkeley, California, personal interview with author, 30 October 1985.

23. Steele interviews.

24. David Halberstam, *The Best and the Brightest* (New York: Random House, 1969), p. 387.

25. John W. Powell, San Francisco, personal interview with author, 27 October 1985.

26. Hugh Deane, "Reporting from China in the 1940s," in *U.S.-China Review* (January-February 1983), pp. 7-8.

27. Steele interviews.

28. Durdin interviews.

29. Raymond Ludden, as cited in Halberstam, *The Best and the Brightest*, p. 111.

30. Steele interviews.

31. Durdin, Steele, and Service interviews.

32. Steele interviews.

33. Durdin interviews.

34. Martin interviews.

35. Steele interviews.

36. Service interview.

37. Barbara W. Tuchman, *Stilwell and the American Experience in China, 1911-1945* (New York: Macmillan, 1971), p. 643.

38. Steele interviews.

39. Service interview.

40. White, *In Search of History*, pp. 77-78.

41. Ibid.

42. White and Jacoby, *Thunder out of China*, p. 248.

43. John F. Melby, *The Mandate of Heaven: Record of a Civil War, China 1945-49* (Toronto: University of Toronto Press, 1968), p. 30.

44. Mike Mansfield, letter to author, received December 1978; Theodore H. White, letter to author, dated September 26, 1978; the copy of White's letter to Luce and other documents relating to Congressman Mansfield's visit to China are on file in the Mike Mansfield Library. See also "'China Mike' Mansfield: The Making of a Congressional Authority on the Far East," by Charles E. Hood, unpublished doctoral dissertation, Washington State University, 1980.

45. White, *In Search of History*, p. 119.

46. Martin interviews.

47. Joseph Stilwell, as cited in White, *In Search of History*, p. 134.

48. Martin interviews.

49. Ibid.

50. Steele interviews.

51. Ibid.

52. Powell interview.

53. Israel Epstein, as reported in Hugh Deane's "Reporting from China in the 1940s," p. 8.

54. Tuchman, *Stilwell and the American Experience in China*, p. 583.

55. Service interview.

56. Hohenberg, *Foreign Correspondents*, p. 371.

57. Deane interview.

58. Durdin interviews.

59. Steele interviews.

60. Melby, *The Mandate of Heaven*, p. 27.

61. Halberstam, *The Best and the Brightest*, p. 11.

62. White, *In Search of History*, p. 209.

63. E. J. Kahn, *The China Hands: America's Foreign Service Officers and What Befell Them* (New York: Viking Press, 1975), p. 18.

64. Fadiman interviews.

65. White, *In Search of History*, p. 209.

66. Steele interviews.

67. Durdin interviews.

68. Martin interviews.

69. Durdin and Steele interviews.

70. "China Editor's Son Has Own Rapier Pen," *Washington Post*, 6 July 1947.

71. "Red China Boy," *Newsweek*, 11 October 1954.

72. Powell interview.

73. Ibid.

74. Ibid.

75. White, *In Search of History*, pp. 261 and 354.

76. Durdin interviews.

77. Fadiman interviews.

78. Phil Potter, as reported in Hugh Deane's "Reporting from China in the 1940s," p. 8.

79. Phillip Knightley, *The First Casualty: From the Crimea to Vietnam— The War Correspondent as Hero, Propagandist, and Myth Maker* (New York: Harcourt, Brace, Jovanovich, 1975), p. 276.

80. Theodore H. White, New York City, telephone interviews with author, 29 October and 16 December 1985.

81. Martin interviews.

82. Tom Engelhardt, "Long Day's Journey: American Observers in China, 1948–50," in *China and Ourselves: Explorations and Revisions by a New Generation*, Bruce Douglass and Ross Terrill (eds.) (Boston: Beacon Press, 1969), pp. 91–121.

83. Deane, "Reporting from China in the 1940s," and Deane interview.

84. Ibid.

85. Deane interview.

86. White interviews.

SELECTIVE BIBLIOGRAPHY

Acheson, Dean. *Present at the Creation: My Years in the State Department.* New York: Norton, 1969.

———. *Private Thoughts on Public Affairs.* New York: Harper and Row, 1967.

Allison, John M. *Ambassador from the Prairie, or Allison Wonderland.* Boston: Houghton Mifflin, 1973.

Ambrose, Stephen. *Eisenhower the President.* New York: Simon and Schuster, 1984.

Aronson, James. *The Press and the Cold War.* Indianapolis: Bobbs-Merrill, 1970.

Bachrack, Stanley. *The Committee of One Million: The China Lobby in American Politics, 1953–71.* New York: Columbia University Press, 1976.

Barrett, David D. *Dixie Mission: The United States Army Observer Group in Yenan, 1944.* Berkeley: Center for Chinese Studies, 1970.

Barth, Alan. *Government by Investigation.* New York: Viking, 1955.

Bemis, Samuel F. (ed.). *The American Secretaries of State and Their Diplomacy,* 10 vols. New York: Pageant Book Co., 1958.

Berman, Larry. *Planning a Tragedy: The Americanization of the War in Vietnam.* New York: Norton, 1982.

Bok, Sissela. *Lying: Moral Choice in Public and Private Life.* New York: Pantheon, 1978.

Borg, Dorothy, and Heinricks, Waldo (eds.). *Uncertain Years: Chinese-American Relations, 1947–1950.* New York: Columbia University Press, 1980.

Buckley, William F., Jr., and Bozell, Brent. *McCarthy and His Enemies.* Chicago: Regnery, 1954.

Buhite, Russell D. *Patrick J. Hurley and American Foreign Policy.* Ithaca: Cornell University Press, 1973.

Cabot, J. M. *First Line of Defense: Fifty Years' Experiences of a Career Diplomat.* Washington, D.C.: Georgetown School of the Foreign Service, n.d.

Caute, David. *The Great Fear: The Anti-Communist Purge Under Truman and Eisenhower.* New York: Simon and Schuster, 1978.

"China." *Time*, 6 January 1986.

Clubb, O. Edmund. *Twentieth Century China.* New York: Columbia University Press, 1978.

_____. *The Witness and I.* New York: Columbia University Press, 1975.

Clyde, Paul H. *United States Policy Toward China: Diplomatic and Public Documents, 1839–1939.* New York: Russell and Russell, 1940.

Davies, John Paton. *Dragon by the Tail: American, British, Japanese, and Russian Encounters with China and One Another.* New York: Norton, 1972.

_____. *Foreign and Other Affairs.* New York: Norton, 1964.

Deane, Hugh. "Reporting from China in the 1940s." *US-China Review* (January-February 1983).

"Documents in the John Paton Davies, Jr., Case." *Foreign Service Journal* (December 1954).

Douglass, Bruce, and Terrill, Ross (eds.). *China and Ourselves: Explorations and Revisions by a New Generation.* Boston: Beacon Press, 1969.

Dulles, Foster Rhea. *American Policy Toward China: The Historical Record.* New York: Crowell, 1972.

Eastman, Lloyd. *Seeds of Destruction: Nationalist China in War and Revolution.* Stanford: Stanford University Press, 1984.

Emmerson, John K. *The Japanese Thread: A Life in the Foreign Service.* New York: Holt, Rinehart, and Winston, 1978.

Fairbank, John King. *The United States and China.* New York: Viking, 1958, ed.

Feis, Herbert. *The China Triangle: The American Effort in China from Pearl Harbor to the Marshall Mission.* Princeton: Princeton University Press, 1953.

Gulick, Edward. *Peter Parker and the Opening of China.* Cambridge: Harvard University Press, 1973.

Hagihara, Nobutoshi, et al. (eds.). *Experiencing the Twentieth Century.* Tokyo: University of Tokyo Press, 1985.

Halberstam, David. *The Best and the Brightest.* New York: Random House, 1969.

Hoffmann, Stanley. *Duties Beyond Borders: On the Limits and Possibilities of Ethical International Politics.* Syracuse: Syracuse University Press, 1981.

Hohenberg, John. *Foreign Correspondence: The Great Reporters and Their Times*. New York: Columbia University Press, 1964.

Hoopes, Townsend. *The Devil and John Foster Dulles: The Diplomacy of the Eisenhower Era*. Boston: Little, Brown, 1973.

Hsu, Immanuel C.Y. *China's Entrance into the Family of Nations: The Diplomatic Phase, 1858–1880*. Cambridge: Harvard University Press, 1960.

————. *The Rise of Modern China*. New York: Oxford University Press, 1970.

Iriye, Akira. *The Cold War in Asia*. Englewood Cliffs: Prentice-Hall, 1974.

"John P. Davies." *Foreign Service Journal* (May 1954).

Jacobs, Dan. *Borodin: Stalin's Man in China*. Cambridge: Harvard University Press, 1981.

————. "Recent Russian Material on Soviet Advisers in China: 1923–1927." *China Quarterly* 41 (January-March 1970).

Kahn, Ely, Jr. *The China Hands: America's Foreign Service Officers and What Befell Them*. New York: Viking, 1975.

Keeley, Joseph. *The China Lobby Man: The Story of Alfred Kohlberg*. New Rochelle: Arlington House, 1969.

Kennan, George. *Memoirs: 1925–1950*. Boston: Little, Brown, 1967.

————. *Memoirs: 1950–1963*. Boston: Little, Brown, 1972.

Knightley, Phillip. *The First Casualty: From the Crimea to Vietnam— The War Correspondent as Hero, Propagandist, and Myth Maker*. New York: Harcourt, Brace, Jovanovich, 1975.

Koen, Ross. *The China Lobby in American Politics*. New York: Harper and Row, 1974.

Kubek, Anthony. *How the Far East Was Lost: American Policy and the Creation of Communist China, 1941–1949*. Chicago: Regnery, 1963.

Latham, Earl. *The Communist Controversy in Washington: From the New Deal to McCarthy*. Cambridge: Harvard University Press, 1966.

Lefever, Ernest W. (ed.). *Ethics and World Politics*. Baltimore: Johns Hopkins University Press, 1972.

Mansfield, Mike. "China Mission Report" Folders, The Mansfield Papers, Series XIX: Personal. University of Montana Archives.

Mao Tse-Tung. *Selected Works*. Peking: Foreign Language Press, 1975.

May, Ernest R. *Lessons of the Past: The Use and Misuse of History in American Foreign Policy*. New York: Oxford University Press, 1973.

May, Gary. *China Scapegoat: The Diplomatic Ordeal of John Carter Vincent*. Washington, D.C.: New Republic Books, 1979.

"The Meaning of the Ruling in the Vincent Case." *Foreign Service Journal* (January 1953).

Melby, John F. *The Mandate of Heaven: Record of a Civil War, China 1945–49.* Toronto: University of Toronto Press, 1968.

_____. "The Origins of the Cold War in China." *Pacific Affairs* (Spring 1968).

Mosley, Leonard. *Dulles: A Biography of Eleanor, Allen, and John Foster Dulles and Their Family Network.* New York: Dial, 1978.

Neils, Patricia. "Henry Luce and American Images of China." *Tamkang Journal of American Studies* 2 (Spring 1986):17–39.

North, Robert, and Eudin, X. M. N. *Roy's Mission to China: The Communist-Kuomintang Split of 1927.* New York: Octagon Books, 1977.

Pelcovits, Nathan. *Old China Hands and the Foreign Office.* New York: King's Crown Press, 1948.

Race, Jeffrey. *War Comes to Long An: Revolutionary Conflict in a Vietnamese Province.* Berkeley: University of California Press, 1972.

"Red China Boy." *Newsweek*, 17 July 1954.

Reeves, Thomas. *The Life and Times of Joe McCarthy.* New York: Stein and Day, 1982.

Rosenberg, Emily. *Spreading the American Dream.* New York: Hill and Wang, 1982.

Schaller, Michael. *The U.S. Crusade in China.* New York: Columbia University Press, 1979.

Seagrave, Sterling. *The Soong Dynasty.* New York: Harper and Row, 1985.

Service, John. *The Amerasia Papers: Some Problems in the History of US-China Relations.* Berkeley: University of California Press, 1971.

_____. "Changes in China, New and Not New." *US-China Review* (July-August 1985).

_____. *Lost Chance in China: The World War II Despatches of John S. Service.* Edited by Joseph W. Esherick. New York: Random House, 1974.

Sevareid, Eric. *Not So Wild a Dream.* New York: Knopf, 1946.

Shai, Aron. *Britain and China: 1941–1947.* New York: St. Martin's Press, 1984.

Shewmaker, Kenneth. *Americans and Chinese Communists, 1927–1947: A Persuading Encounter.* Ithaca: Cornell University Press, 1971.

Snow, Edgar. *The Other Side of the River: Red China Today.* New York: Random House, 1962.

_____. *Red Star over China.* New York: Grove Press, 1961 ed.

Terrill, Ross. "When America 'Lost' China." *The Atlantic*, November 1969.

Thies, Wallace. *When Governments Collide: Coercion and Diplomacy in the Vietnam Conflict, 1964–1968.* Berkeley: University of California Press, 1980.

Thomson, James C., Jr. "China Reporting Revisited." *Nieman Reports* (Spring 1983).

———. *While China Faced West.* Cambridge: Harvard University Press, 1969.

Tong, Te-kong. *United States Diplomacy in China, 1844–1860.* Seattle: University of Washington Press, 1964.

Tsou, Tang. *America's Failure in China: 1941–1950.* Chicago: University of Chicago Press, 1963.

Tuchman, Barbara. *The March of Folly.* New York: Knopf, 1984.

———. *Stilwell and the American Experience in China, 1911–1945.* New York: Macmillan, 1971.

Tucker, Nancy. *Patterns in the Dust.* New York: Columbia University Press, 1983.

United States. Congress. Senate. Committee on Foreign Relations. *The Evolution of U.S. Policy Toward Mainland China.* Washington, D.C.: Government Printing Office, 1971.

———. *State Department Employee Loyalty Investigation.* Washington, D.C.: Government Printing Office, 1950.

———. *U.S. Policy with Respect to Mainland China.* Washington, D.C.: Government Printing Office, 1966.

United States. Department of State. *Foreign Relations of the United States, 1944.* Volume VI, *China.* Washington, D.C.: Government Printing Office, 1967.

———. *Foreign Relations of the United States, 1945.* Volume VII, *The Far East: China.* Washington, D.C.: Government Printing Office, 1969.

———. *Foreign Relations of the United States, 1947.* Volume VII, *The Far East: China.* Washington, D.C.: Government Printing Office, 1972.

———. *United States Relations with China, with Special Reference to the Period 1944–1949.* Washington, D.C.: Government Printing Office, 1949.

Utley, Freda. *The China Story.* Chicago: Regnery, 1951.

Van Slyke, Lyman P. (ed.). *The China White Paper, August 1949.* Stanford: Stanford University Press, 1967.

———. *The Chinese Communist Movement: A Report of the United States War Department, July 1945.* Stanford: Stanford University Press, 1968.

Vishnyakova-Akimova, Vera. *Two Years in Revolutionary China, 1925–1927.* Steven Levine (trans.). Cambridge: East Asian Research Center, Harvard University, 1971.

Wedemeyer, Albert. *Wedemeyer Reports!* New York: Holt, 1958.

Weinstein, Allen. *Perjury: The Hiss-Chambers Case.* New York: Knopf, 1978.

White, Theodore. *In Search of History: A Personal Adventure.* New York: Harper and Row, 1978.

———. (ed.). *The Stilwell Papers.* New York: Sloane, 1948.

White, Theodore, and Jacoby, Annalee. *Thunder out of China.* New York: Sloan, 1946.

Wilbur, C. Martin, and How, Julie (eds.). *Documents on Communism, Nationalism, and Soviet Advisers in China, 1918–1927.* Cambridge: Harvard University Press, 1981.

Wolfers, Arnold. "Statesmanship and Moral Choice," in *Discord and Collaboration: Essays on International Politics.* Baltimore: Johns Hopkins University Press, 1962.

ABOUT THE CONTRIBUTORS

John Paton Davies. Born in Kiating, China, of American missionary parents, Davies earned his degree at Columbia University in New York and then joined the Foreign Service. He became one of the best known of the "China Hands" and served in a number of Chinese cities, including Kunming, Peking, Mukden, Hankow, and Chungking. During World War II he was political adviser to General Joseph Stilwell, commanding general of the U.S. Forces in the China-India-Burma Theater. In this capacity, he visited the Chinese Communists in their wartime capital of Yenan. He won the Medal of Freedom following a parachute jump into the Burmese jungles. After the war he served in the Soviet Union and Germany and on the Policy Planning Staff of the Department of State. His long experience in China made him a target for Senator Joseph McCarthy, who accused Davies of being one of the professional diplomats responsible for "losing" China to the Communists. Secretary of State John Foster Dulles fired him in 1954. His security clearance was restored only in 1964. Davies is the author of *Foreign and Other Affairs* and *Dragon by the Tail*.

Charles Hood. A recipient of bachelor's and master's degrees from the University of Montana and a Ph.D. in American studies from Washington State University, Hood worked as a newsman for a number of years. In this capacity he wrote for several newspapers and United Press International and won awards from the National Headliners Club, the American Medical Association, the Association of Trial Lawyers, and the Society of Professional Journalists. His articles have appeared in *Editor and Publisher* and *The Montana Journalism Review*. He is working on a biography of Mike Mansfield. Hood is presently the Dean of the University of Montana School of Journalism.

Immanuel C.Y. Hsu. A native of Shanghai, Hsu earned a bachelor's degree from Yenching University in Peking and then a Ph.D. from Harvard University. He has been a member of the history faculty at the University of California, Santa Barbara, since 1959. In 1971 he was designated a faculty research lecturer, his university's highest faculty distinction. Professor Hsu has received Guggenheim and Fulbright fellowships and returned to China in 1983 by the National Academy of Sciences as a distinguished scholar. He is the author of several books, including *China Without Mao: The Search for a New Order* and *China's Entrance into the Family of Nations*. His book, *The Rise of Modern China*, won the Commonwealth Literary Prize of California in 1971.

Akira Iriye. Iriye was born in Japan and received his doctorate in United States and Far Eastern history from Harvard University. He has taught at Harvard, the University of California at Santa Cruz, the University of Rochester, and the University of California at Berkeley. He joined the faculty of the University of Chicago in 1969 and has been chairman of the Department of History since 1979. In 1983 Iriye was named Distinguished Service Professor of American Diplomatic History. He is chairman of the Committee on American-East Asian Relations of the American Historical Association. He has written eight books, including *After Imperialism, Pacific Estrangement, The Cold War in Asia*, and *Power and Culture: The Japanese-American War, 1941–1945*. He won Japan's Yoshida Shigeru Prize for the best book in the field of international relations in 1979.

Paul Gordon Lauren. Lauren earned his Ph.D. from Stanford University where he was a Woodrow Wilson Fellow and where he has taught on several occasions. He joined the Department of History at the University of Montana in 1974. Lauren has been a National Peace Fellow, a Social Science Research Council Fellow, and a Rockefeller Foundation Humanities Fellow. Lauren has published two books, *Diplomacy: New Approaches in History, Theory, and Policy* and *Diplomats and Bureaucrats*, and has just completed another on the politics and diplomacy of human rights. His articles have appeared in *Diplomatic History, International Studies Quarterly, Journal of Conflict Resolution, International History Review*, and *Human Rights Quarterly*. He presently is the Director and Professor of Ethics and Public Affairs of the Maureen and Mike Mansfield Center at the University of Montana.

Ernest R. May. May received his doctorate from the University of California at Los Angeles and shortly thereafter began teaching at Harvard University. He was dean of Harvard College from 1969 to 1971, director of the Institute of Politics from 1971 to 1974, and chairman of the Department of History from 1976 to 1979. He was named Charles Warren Professor of History in 1981. Professor May is a member of the Council on Foreign Relations and a fellow of the American Academy of Arts and Sciences. His books include *The World War and American Isolation, 1914–1917*, for which he won the George Louis Beer Prize of the American Historical Association in 1959; *The Ultimate Decision: The President as Commander-in-Chief*; *Imperial Democracy*; *American Imperialism*; and *Lessons of the Past: The Use and Misuse of History in American Foreign Policy*.

John Fremont Melby. Melby received his doctorate from the University of Chicago. He served in the Foreign Service, including an assignment in China. He was director of the U.S. Educational Foundation in China in 1948 and chairman of military assistance missions to the Philippines and Southeast Asia from 1949 to 1950. He was the principal author of *United States Relations with China*, known as the famous China White Paper, in 1949. His other books include *The Mandate from Heaven: Record of a Civil War, China 1945–1949*. In 1966 Professor Melby became chairman of the Department of Political Studies at the University of Guelph in Ontario, Canada. Now a professor emeritus, he continues to teach and conduct research.

John W. Powell. Born in Shanghai as the son of a famous American journalist, Powell was educated at the Missouri School of Journalism. He worked in 1940 as a newsman in China before joining the U.S. Office of War Information as an editor at the outset of World War II. In 1943 he was assigned to China. From 1945 to 1953 he edited the *China Weekly Review* in Shanghai and was described in the American press as "a fearless newspaperman" and one of the best informed journalists in China. Upon returning to the United States in the midst of McCarthyism, however, he rapidly found himself being charged with sedition and treason because of his critical articles. The charges were eventually dropped. Powell currently lives in San Francisco where he continues to write about Asian affairs.

Raymond F. Wylie. Wylie is the Maureen and Mike Mansfield Professor of Modern Asian Affairs at the Mansfield Center, University of Montana. He is also a member of a number of professional societies, including the Royal Institute of International Affairs, London. He has a broad interest in international relations and East Asia and specializes in the field of Chinese politics and foreign policy. Wylie has written extensively on various aspects of modern China; his works include *The Emergence of Maoism, 1935–45*, published by Stanford University Press in 1980. In addition his articles have appeared in the *Bulletin of the Atomic Scientists*, the *China Quarterly*, the *Far Eastern Economic Review,* and other academic publications.

THE MAUREEN AND MIKE MANSFIELD CENTER

The Maureen and Mike Mansfield Center at the University of Montana is designed to recognize and honor the Mansfields' public service contributions over more than four decades. The inspiration for the Center derives from Mike Mansfield's distinguished career and the two subjects with which he has long been identified: a staunch commitment to high ethical standards in public affairs and insightful contributions to the nation's Asian policies. Ethics and Public Affairs and Modern Asian Affairs thus form the Mansfield Center's two principal programs.

Mike Mansfield's outstanding and inspiring reputation as a public official is based on his numerous achievements and personal qualities. Both he and his wife, Maureen, whom he always credits as being responsible for many of his successes, are graduates of the University of Montana. He served as a faculty member in the Department of History and then represented the people of the state of Montana for ten years in the House of Representatives and for twenty-four in the Senate. He served as Senate Majority Leader longer than anyone else in American history. President Jimmy Carter appointed Mike Mansfield as the U.S. ambassador to Japan in 1977. His retirement from the Senate in 1976 was the occasion for one of the greatest outpourings of esteem ever given a departing senator by his colleagues, who commented about his "special expertise in the area of foreign policy," "grasp of international issues," "immense knowledge of East Asia," and, above all, his "character and integrity." Mike Mansfield served as "the conscience" of the Senate, setting "an inspiring example of the very highest standards of principled public service" and exercising "a moral leadership which reflects the ideals and finest traditions of our country." As one senator felt compelled to say, "Honor, decency, fairness, tolerance—these have been his hallmarks—and those qualities, much more than our words in praise of him, will remain his most eloquent tributes."

The educational programs of the Center seek to reach a variety of groups and interests. Its undergraduate courses on Ethics and Public Affairs and Modern Asian Affairs are open to students from many different disciplines. Outstanding graduate students, known as Mansfield Fellows, will be provided with generous assistance and unique opportunities to complete their degree programs. The Center will fund research, visiting scholars, and a summer fellows program. Each year the Burlington Northern Foundation supports a major public conference devoted to one of the Center's two areas of concentration.

The Ethics and Public Affairs program focuses on the relationship of values to public institutions offering instruction on ethical dimensions of public policies and governmental service. The Modern Asian Affairs program provides courses and seminars on Asian affairs and language instruction for students who have a vocational or academic interest in Asia. Initial courses deal with modern intellectual, social, and political developments in Asia.

INDEX